ALBERTA ALBUM
THE LIVING PAST

ALBERTA ALBUM
THE LIVING PAST

David Cunningham
David Sternthal
Principal Photography

Carl Betke
General Editor

W. Mark Giles
Editor

Copyright © 1985 by Lone Pine Publishing
© 1985 Alberta Culture

First Printing 1985   5 4 3 2 1

Printed in Canada

All rights reserved.

No part of this book may be reproduced in any
form without permission in writing from the
publishers, except by a reviewer who may quote
brief passages in a magazine or newspaper.

The Publishers
Lone Pine Publishing   Alberta Culture
#414 10357 109 St.
Edmonton, Alberta T5J 1N3

Typesetting by Pièce de Résistance
Typographers, Edmonton

Printed by Commerical Color Press Ltd., Edmonton

Canadian Cataloguing in Publication Data

Cunningham, Dave, 1951-
  Alberta album

  Co-publishing by Alberta Culture.
  ISBN 0-919433-44-8

  1. Historic sites - Alberta. 2. Alberta - History.
3. Alberta - Description and travel - 1981-
4. Historic sites - Alberta - Pictorial works.
5. Alberta - Description and travel - 1981-
Views. I. Sternthal, David. II. Giles, W. Mark. III.
Alberta. Alberta Culture. IV. Title.
FC3662.C85 1985   971.23   C85-091609-7
F1076.8.C85 1985

This book is dedicated to the sons and daughters of the men and women who built Alberta. Indians, explorers, traders, pioneers, immigrants, roughnecks, refugees—dreamers all.

CREDITS

A few years ago, Frits Pannekoek, Director of the Historic Sites Service, Alberta Culture, conceived of a book which would introduce Alberta's designated historic sites. Following his initiative, and eventually under the direction of Carl Betke, the Historic Sites Service staff in consultation with the Archaeological Survey of Alberta and the Provincial Museum of Alberta, compiled, checked, refined and edited the information which would explain the background of each site designated up until 1982. Identifying photographs were collected, many of them produced under the supervision of Michael Carley, and supplemented by the work of volunteer photographer Edward Thomson.

The search for a means of presentation eventually led to the development of several concepts by Grant Kennedy at Lone Pine Publishing. It was he who argued persuasively for a book which would surpass the mere compilation of a record of Alberta's historic sites with an evocation of their character and their capacity to inspire reflection and understanding. The result was a decision to highlight expressive views of Alberta's built and written record, to provide the reader with a sample of the rich and intricate experience associated with Alberta's historic sites.

In a co-publishing agreement with Alberta Culture, Lone Pine Publishing engaged Prairie Wool Communications and photographers David Cunningham and David Sternthal to supply a comprehensive range of colour photographs. From the 2,000 pictures were selected a few dozen that best reflected Alberta's heritage.

Freelance writer and researcher Janice E. MacDonald was given the task of unearthing historical quotations to furnish a vivid echo of the voices and activities which helped to shape Alberta's modern society. Acknowledgement must be made to Historic Sites Service staff (who helped Janice), The Provincial Archives of Alberta, The Glenbow-Alberta Institute, The Bruce Peel Memorial Special Collections at The University of Alberta Library, and John Mount of Alberta Culture—Visual Arts.

Such a highly visual and "unwritten" book such as *Alberta Album* demands a great deal of effort from many. Thanks to Al Shute, Bob Young and Sharon McIntyre for their pre-production work. Thanks to illustrators David Marko, Sheryl Caldwell, Anthony Cranfield-Rose and Jaime Romero.

In addition to David Cunningham and David Sternthal, Prairie Wool Communications employed photographers Dave Jordan, Dale Jarhaus, and Kim Pudde. Additional photographs were chosen from the work of freelance photographers Ian Scott, Jeff Fleetham and Bonnie Bentley. Colour prints courtesy of K. Jack Clark Photography & Lab Services, Edmonton. Colour separations by Barry Benjamin of the Graphic Edge, Edmonton.

Typeset by Pièce de Résistance Graphics. Printed by Commercial Colour Press (special thanks to Gord Salway). Bound by The Northwest Book Company, Vancouver.

Principal Photography by
David Cunningham
PRAIRIE WOOL COMMUNICATIONS
David Sternthal
PRAIRIE WOOL COMMUNICATIONS

Contributing Photographers:
Bonnie Bentley, Dale Jarhaus,
Dave Jordan, Jeff Fleetham,
Kim Pudde, Ian Scott and Darryl Snaychuk.

General Editor
Carl Betke
ALBERTA CULTURE

Editor
W. Mark Giles
LONE PINE PUBLISHING

Art Director
Ed Kusiak
LONE PINE PUBLISHING

Research
Janice E. MacDonald

Historic Sites Compilation —
Researchers and writers
Douglas Babcock
Margaret Barry
Radomir Bilash
John Gilpin
Les Hurt
Charles Mandel
David May
Jane McCracken
Ron Mussieux
Patricia Myers
Rod Vickers

Historic Sites Compilation —
Photographers
Judy Bedford
Michael Carley
Stephen Evin
Garnett Smith
Edward Thomson
Klaas Vink

Maps
Andre Lafleur
Gwendolyn Lefsrud
Lillian Wonders

CONTENTS

Introduction 13

Call of the North 15

Peace 27

Gateway to the North 43

Hallowed Hills / Shining Mountains 65

Where the Elbow Meets the Bow 85

Big Sky 105

Grasslands 129

Historic Sites of Alberta 141

INTRODUCTION

The modern mind has become accustomed to witnessing swift replacement. What is familiar to the elderly is forgotten history to the young. People moving to Alberta or visiting for the first time are often struck by the relative newness of the province. The same observation has been made again and again for 200 years—Alberta is always new, always changing. The changes leave more than a memory. To understand the nature of Alberta today is to interpret the signs of human energy on a landscape in transition.

The past did not begin with the establishment of the province in 1905, nor with the arrival of the railroad, nor with the exploration of Anthony Henday in 1754. Before there were historians here to record it, history—both human and natural—was developing. The strangeness of human prehistory and the difficulty of its recovery may at times hamper our understanding of people, events and places before the time of recorded history. Blended in time with the ponderous, irresistible processes of natural change, the archaeological clues to the past require painstaking study. By sifting through the layers of a centuries-old buffalo jump or a medicine wheel, archaeologists gain insights into the harmonious and changing integration of human action with the surrounding landscape.

Yet it is not necessary to look into the hoary depths of prehistory in order to comprehend how the visible past was conditioned by the historical environment. Whether examining the configurations of tepee rings on the southern plains, or mapping the quadrant layout of Edmonton's streets, we can see the special social preconceptions which defined their design.

The prehistory of Alberta was a gradual evolution of nature and man. The recorded history of Alberta is an explosive record of human development. The relative newness of most of Alberta's historical resources belies the ancient traditions—both native and foreign—that led to their development. Churches less than a century old reflect age-old patterns of worship and architectural codification. The earliest commercial and industrial structures built in the pre-World War I boom were extensions of the same motivation which led the first Europeans to North America a half-millenium ago. Even the building of the railroads constituted not only an act of political will and geographical union, but a physical linking from the regions of old dreams to a land of new opportunities and ambitions. Traders, explorers, Indians, pioneers and dreamers all arrived in Alberta in search of something—and they created something new.

It is perhaps too easy to underestimate the importance of Alberta's historical resources. After all, ours is a short past—certainly a house or a coal mine a few decades old cannot be as significant as Egypt's pyramids, the Athenian Acropolis or the Forum of Rome. Yet history is not a quantifiable resource. Antiquity does not translate directly into worth. Structural remains of Alberta's relics reveal the complex network of relationships that existed among the many diverse individuals and communities within the province. The remains of fur trade posts recall the unique economy that at once defined European action in the land and at the same time changed the behaviour of the natives. The varieties of pioneer home and farmstead construction reflect the multicultural origins of the later settlers and the uneasy synthesis that resulted from the rapid diffusion of many different cultures. Alberta's short past streams and spills into the present to give us a glimpse of what may come.

Alberta Album presents a photographic record of our province's relics—some forgotten, some revitalized and all bursting with the stuff of history. To this modern record are tuned the voices of the past—the oral and written words of those who fashioned the intricate character of a proud province. It is a record of individual and collective effort that adapted to and transformed the land. As it did with our forefathers, Alberta continues to beckon to succeeding generations with opportunities rooted in the land and its resources. *Alberta Album* is a mirror to yesterday, and a window on today.

CALL OF THE NORTH

Anthony Henday, Peter Pond, Peter Pangman, David Thompson, Peter Fidler and Alexander Mackenzie — these legendary names from Canada's past evoke the spirit of exploration and discovery. The first white man to set foot in what is now Alberta crossed the Fourth Principal Meridian in 1754. But the white man's influence had preceded Anthony Henday. Up the rivers from Hudson Bay, the eastern Cree and Assiniboine tribes had been encroaching on the lands to the west, bartering European-made trinkets and tools picked up from The Company of Gentlemen Adventurers from England Trading into Hudson's Bay. The rush to Alberta was on.

It seems odd today that Alberta's empty quarter, the vast and sparsely populated lands of the northeast, was the focus of earliest explorations. Across the Methy

The northern dusk falls over the Catholic Church at St. Paul.

DAVID CUNNINGHAM

Portage, down the Clearwater and Athabasca rivers, and up the mighty Peace came the vanguard of traders pouring into the north. Iroquois Indians, Orkney Island labourers and French-Canadian voyageurs were among these earliest immigrants. Some, like American Peter Pond, coveted the furry wealth of the virgin forests. Others, like the Scot Alexander Mackenzie, sought the Northwest Passage to oriental riches.

However, history has proven fickle. Fort Chipewyan, Alberta's first non-native settlement (and permanently inhabited since the 1790s) remains remote and lonely on the distant shores of Lake Athabasca. A century after the fur trade boom, pioneers snapped up the only arable land between the Athabasca and North Saskatchewan rivers. Today, north of the fields first broken by French-Canadian, Ukrainian and other homesteaders near Bonnyville, Lac La Biche and Athabasca, the edge of agriculture peters out into the black spruce of untamed boreal forest. The city of Fort McMurray with its high-technology oil sands refineries stands as a modern oasis of thriving industry in the midst of the wilderness. The northeast was Alberta's first frontier. It still challenges the adventurous.

Fort Chipewyan and Lake Athabasca.

Among the Clerks of this last Company, was a Mr. Peter Pond, a native of the city of Boston, United States. He was a person of industrious habits, a good common education, but of a violent temper and unprincipled character; his place was at Fort Chipewyan on the north side of the Athabasca Lake, where he wintered three years.
—*David Thompson in* TRAVELS IN WESTERN NORTH AMERICA 1784-1812.

A York boat at sunset. York boats carried the bulk of traffic on the rivers during the fur trade.

DAVID CUNNINGHAM

Log cabin near Bonnyville.

I have however got far out of the expedition track & must return to the excavated channel of upper Peace River, which lays open the horizontal layers that forms the Plains of Peace river at least to some hundred feet as before mentioned & which consists of Thick Layers of colored Moulds Gravel, Sand Clay, Ochers, Stone from 1 Inch Thick to many feet, generally like indurated Clays & mixture, sand stone & also of the Coal formations pretty plentiful & on fire in Smoky River also at one place near Dunvegan & the petrefaction process also seems active in some places & quantities of recent formation of stone & some shells & other Fossils &c found petrified also Carbonic & spar productions. We also see the appearance of Sulphur & Iron & a kind of Sulphrates or Iron production found in the Bed of the River very ponderous & seem recent formation— moreover the Earths &c in Peace River is strongly impregnated with Salts besides the Thick layers of Stone we see (generally under the Earth layers) in the Banks of Peace River.
—*Samuel Black's* JOURNAL, *1824.*

The forerunner to today's massive developments in the Fort McMurray area, the Bitumount refinery was built to process the Athabasca Tar Sands in 1930.

Sam Q. Brown
Philadelphia

Dec. 19, 1882

The Chester Oil Company, Philadelphia
Sam Q. Brown, Treasurer

Robt. Bell Esq. M.D.
Ottawa, Canada
My Dear Sir,
  I have only time to acknowlege your note 11th last. I know nothing about the indication of petroleum in Athabasca region further than contained in your letter. Petroleum indications at best are very uncertain. It strikes me even if good territory should be developed, it will be a long time before transportation facilities would justify its developments....

Sincerely,
Sam Q. Brown

—As head of the Geological Survey of Canada, Robert Bell did early research into the economic viability of the Athabasca Tar Sands.

A rusting binder finds its final resting place in a field near Waugh.

The onion dome of the St. Mary's Ukrainian Church bespeaks the heritage of the area's settlers.

In the course of the afternoon we passed one or two deserted tents, and "sweating booths," but no Indians. . . . The "sweating booths" referred to should have been explained before. They are the great Indian natural luxury, and are to be found all along the road, or wherever Indians live even for a week. There was scarcely a day this month that we did not pass the rude slight frames. At first we mistook them for small tents. They are made in a few minutes of willow wands or branches, bent so as to form a circular enclosure, with room for one or two inside; the buffalo robe is spread over the framework so as to exclude the air as much as possible, and whoever wants a Russian bath crawls into the round dark hole. A friend outside then heats some large stones to the highest point attainable, and passes them and a bucket of water in. The "insides" pour the water on the stones, steam is generated, and, on they go pouring water and enjoying the delight of a vapor bath, till they are almost insensible. Doctor Hector thought the practice an excellent one, as regards cleanliness, health and pleasure; but the Indians carry it to an extreme that utterly enervates them. Their medicine-men enlist it in aid of their superstitions. It is when under the influence of the bath, that they become inspired; and they take one or two laymen in with them, that they

Willow framework for a "sweating booth."

may hear their oracular sayings, and be able to announce to the tribe where there is a chance of stealing horses or of doing some other notable deed with good prospect of success. It is easy to see, too, what a capital opportunity the medicine-man has, when thus inspired to gratify his private malice or vengeance, or any desire. Many a raid and many a deed of darkness has been started in the sweating booth.

—*Rev. George M. Grant,* SANFORD FLEMING'S EXPEDITION THROUGH CANADA IN 1872.

North West Mounted Police,
Athabasca Landing,
21st April, 1904.

To the Officer Commanding,
N.W.M. Police
Fort Saskatchewan.

Sir,

I have the honour to make the following report of this Detachment for the week ending April 21st, 1904:

Customs . . . . Nil
Cattle . . . . Looking well
Game . . . . Plentiful
Indians . . . . Quiet
Livery Stables . . . . Well kept
New settlers . . . . Nil
Prairie fires . . . . Nil
Rivers . . . . High
Trails . . . . Bad
Shoeing and general state of horses . . . . Good

—Weekly report form H. Haslett, Sergeant-in-charge.

The end of an era — Athabasca Landing. Athabasca was a major shipping terminal for goods moving north in the late 1800s and early 1900s.

Abandoned lineshack on the old trail to Athabasca Landing.

The Gentlemen of Fort Chipewean are making their Gardens on the bed of the Lake, between Rocky Hills that were not perhaps very long ago Rocky Islands in the Lake, but whether these are the productions of before or after the Flood or a gradual decrease of the aquatic element observed all over the Country, Lakes & Marches turning into dry Land &c, I shall leave the Philosophers to determine.
—*From Samuel Black's* JOURNAL, *September 1824. Ft. Chipewyan was the first permanent European settlement in Alberta.*

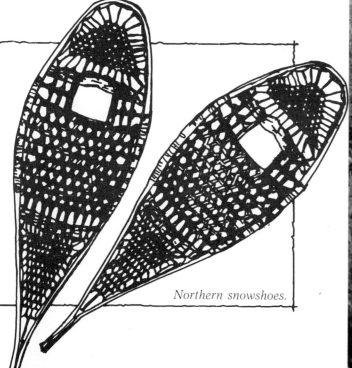

Northern snowshoes.

DAVID CUNNINGHAM

DAVID CUNNINGHAM

DAVID CUNNINGHAM

DAVID CUNNINGHAM

Top left
Grandin House, St. Albert.
Bottom left
Convent at Morinville.
Right
Morinville Catholic Church.

PEACE

The Peace River dominates all aspects of northwestern Alberta — the geography, the history, the economics, even the culture. The wide green valley streams through the north like a verdant swatch of fertile prairie stitched across the black spruce forests. Because of its bounty, crops of wheat are grown as far north as Fort Vermilion. Trappers still comb its banks and tributaries in search of valuable pelts.

The river's serene name was given by the Indians before the first European ever paddled its waters, yet the Hudson's Bay Company was the influence behind the name. Early in the 18th century the powerful Cree nation enjoyed singular wealth. They were the middle-men to Hudson Bay, and were moving ever westward. With their guns and superior tools, they pushed the traditional inhabitants of the Peace

"Wings over Peace." A bush plane (top right) prepares to land while the sun sets over the Peace River.

JEFF FLEETHAM

River valley and delta, the Beaver Indians, further up river. When the Beaver and Cree settled their dispute in the 1760s (at Peace Point

in Wood Buffalo National Park), they named the river as a monument to their lasting peace.

The heroes of Alberta's northwest are giants in the land they tamed. Sir George Simpson, Bishop Emile Grouard, George Dawson, Henry "Twelve Foot" Davis and "Peace River Jim" Cornwall are among those who inspired larger-than-life legends. They and other northwestern pioneers had to struggle up the Athabasca, across Lesser Slave Lake and through the 80-mile boggy bush to reach *la grande prairie*. The Peace River district was the last great opportunity in Alberta for homesteading, and the hardy few who ventured north soon found that early frosts and distant markets would challenge them as much as the muskegs and isolation. Today, northwestern Alberta still thrums with the rugged spirit of the pioneer.

The Hudson's Bay Co. post at Dunvegan was one of the most important in the north.

DAVID JORDAN

Sunday, 11th May, 1828

Arrived here the ninth day (from Fort Vermilion) about 1 o'clock p.m. in a large canoe, much embarrassed with goods, food, private property, etc. etc. The crew—Bte. Lafleur, Interpreter, I. Bte. Errand Engage, Ber Mannville (a Ft. Vermilion man who came to assist us up and is to return immediately), Charles LeFleur and A. Pagé freeman and a Beaver Indian—Passengers—C. Campbell and family consisting of woman and six children. Found the buildings in a very ruinous condition—numerous tracks of buffalos, moose, etc. around the fort.

15 May

All hands busily employed about the garden, repairing the most tenable of the buildings to store the company's property and to lodge ourselves.

27 August 1828

In the afternoon was agreeably surprised by the arrival of the two canoes manned by 19 men—being Governor Simpson on his way to the Columbia via New Caledonia.

16 January 1830

Our two Fort Hunters arrived & report of having killed 53 Buffalos—a great many more than we want & they are not fat enough to make dried provision, so that the meat will be lost. The snow is so very deep that all large animals cannot run from the pursuers & there will be no doubt a great number wantonly killed. Although I do my best by persuasion to prevent it.

—From the journal of Robert Campbell, who re-established the trading post at Dunvegan after the amalgamation of the Hudson's Bay Co. and the Northwest Co.

28

A homestead near Manning. Though in the north of the Peace River Block, the Manning area attracted many settlers after 1911.

JEFF FLEETHAM

Lesser Slave Lake. Peace River pioneers faced a tortuous journey over the Athabasca Landing Trail, then up the Athabasca and across Lesser Slave Lake, and finally an 80-mile trek through treacherous muskeg to the Peace Country.

Advertisement from THE CALGARY EYE OPENER, *1912.*

The railway station in the town of Peace River. Without a railway to move produce to markets, the rich Peace River valley would have no agricultural industry.

Edmonton, Dunvegan and British Columbia Rly.

DINING CAR SERVICE

Luncheon and Evening Meal

MIXED PICKLES, 15c   OLIVES, 20c   CHOW CHOW, 15c

SOUPS, 25c
(Served to order, 10 minutes)
(See Special Slip)

FISH, 65c
(See Special Slip)

BROILED OR FRIED MEATS

SIRLOIN STEAK, $1.25   SMALL SIRLOIN STEAK, 90c
GRILLED LAMB CHOPS, (1) 45c; (2) 80c; (with Bacon or Tomato Sauce, 15c extra)
BACON, (2 STRIPS) 20c; (3 STRIPS) 30c   SUGAR-CURED HAM (FULL CUT) 65c
HAM OR BACON WITH TWO FRIED EGGS, 65c
FRIED CALF'S LIVER WITH BACON, 55c   SMALL COUNTRY SAUSAGES (6), 55c
(With Mashed Potatoes, 65c)
BAKED BEANS, (Hot or Cold) 35c

ROASTS
(See Special Slip)

COLD MEATS

HAM, 65c   MUTTON, 45c   TONGUE, 65c   BEEF, 70c   CHICKEN, 90c
WITH POTATO SALAD, 10c EXTRA

EGGS, OMELETTES, Etc.

BOILED OR FRIED EGGS, (2) 30c   POACHED ON TOAST, 40c   SCRAMBLED, (2) 35c
OMELETTES, PLAIN, 45c   JELLY OR PARSLEY, 60c   CHEESE OR TOMATO, 50c

SALADS
(See Special Slip)

VEGETABLES

POTATOES

BOILED, 15c   MASHED, 15c   FRENCH FRIED, 25c   HASHED BROWN, 25c
(10 Minutes)   (10 Minutes)

GREEN PEAS, 20c   SWEET CORN, 20c   STEWED TOMATOES, 20c
FRESH VEGETABLES (See Special Slip)

DESSERT

PRESERVED FRUITS, 25c   JAM, MARMALADE OR JELLY, 25c
CANADIAN STILTON CHEESE WITH TOASTED CRACKERS, 25c
PLAIN, GRAHAM OR FRUIT BREAD AND BUTTER (per person) 10c   ROLLS, 15c
DRY OR BUTTERED TOAST, 15c
TEA OR COFFEE (Per Pot) 20c
COCOA, (cup) 20c; (Per Pot) 25c   MILK (Per Glass) 15c

No Order Served for Less than 25c to Each Person

A menu from the original Edmonton, Dunvegan and British Columbia Railway, 1915. The E.D. & B.C. (nicknamed "Exceedingly Dangerous and Badly Constructed") reached Peace River in 1914.

The cemetery at St. Bernard's Mission at Grouard.

The St. Jean Baptiste Mission, near Falher.

Steeple detail of St. Jean Baptiste Mission.

IAN SCOTT

H.F. DAVIS

Born in Vermont, 1820
Died at Slave Lake, 1893
Pathfinder, Pioneer,
Miner and Trader
He Was Every Man's Friend
And Never Locked
His Cabin Door

The epitaph on the grave of Henry "Twelve-Foot" Davis. He actually died in 1900, not 1893.

Yesterday's window.

A 1911 federal election pamphlet inscribed in Cree (for the Lesser Slave Lake district). The inventor of the Cree syllabic alphabet, the Wesleyan Reverend James Evans, was the first missionary to visit the Slave Lake and Peace River districts in 1841.

"We marched jauntily down the roadway and back down the Midway on each side of which were restaurants, a refreshment booth and dance pavillion. People, dogs and teepees everywhere and back in the bush at the side was the tom-tom. I had to see that tent and peeped in. They were gambling— with their hands under quilts. One man exposed while I was there, both hands in one of which a quarter lay. Tom-tom beat and man beating it sang "Ia-Ia-yah!" and all who squatted in tent shook with excitement, whilst the drummer actually wriggled."
—*Rev. John McDougall, near Grouard, Diary 1909.*

Bishop Grandin House, St. Albert.

Old barn near Waugh.

"I went there [Peace River district] to keep house for George for awhile. Everyone was feeling so sorry for me because I'd just got word that Milton was killed in the army; I was engaged to him. So, to get away from it I went to see George, and I stayed.

Well, I came up to the Peace River country. My brother George came all the way to Grande Prairie to meet me, the train didn't go any further than that. We drove out to Beaverlodge and the next day was the 24th of May, and they had all the Sports. So I went to the Sports that day with him and there was a ball game on and this little short guy with a peaked hat on playing ball and George introduces him to me and he takes his little hat off and bows down to the ground like this, he's an American you know with his "Pleased to meet you." That night we had a dance and I took him for a Ladies' Choice and after that he was my boyfriend.

He [Homer] asked me if I wanted to get married and I said I guess I would, and then he wanted to know about a ring, because Pauline had got a diamond ring from Gord, so he said "Would you like a diamond?" He said, "You can either have a diamond or a new stove," you know because they only had little box stoves in those days, so I said I'd take the stove. I didn't want to use the little wee box stoves like the rest were using, with no oven on it. So I got a nice range for the price that a diamond ring would be, or was then. It cost seventy-five dollars.

When I first came up to be with my brother George the flu broke out that winter. I came up and I nursed George all the way through, he was upstairs in bed, and everytime I went up to his room I wore a mask. And I wore a mask when I went into town, everybody was wearing masks to keep from getting the germs I guess. I had formaldehyde, a tin of formaldehyde on the stove all the time to keep from getting the germs. I'd put a little drop of formaldehyde on my mask, so I'd smell it. And I never caught it.

Billy Johnson lived on the next quarter and every day he'd walk over to see if I was all right. And I never caught it. I went in and Mr. and Mrs. Bond who run the post office there, he was a minister, and he was down with it and she caught it too, so I went in and looked after her. And then I went down to see Homer, I remember riding down on horseback to see how he was. I heard they all had the flu down there."

—Interview with Mrs. Louise Jaque (born 1892) who homesteaded in Lower Beaverlodge.

Window detail of log cabin near Athabasca.

Regarding the Beaver Indians. Their old enemies were the Woods Crees. About seven miles out on the Spirit River Trail is an open place called ''Resting Knoll,'' where the Beavers used to wait until the Crees came up and then they would fight.

Spirit River [is] called so for the people killed in these battles; their spirits were supposed to hover around the district river.
—*Rev. John McDougall, Diary July 1909*

A subdued late evening sun, dimmed by the smoke from many fires burning in the northern forests.

October 9th

A Highlander of the name Colin Frazer had joined our party. He was on his way to a small post, of which he had the charge, at the head of the Athabasca River, in the Rocky Mountains, where he had resided for the last eleven years. He had been brought to the country by Sir George Simpson, in the capacity of his piper, at the time when he explored Frazer's River, and made an extensive voyage through a country hitherto little known, and among Indians who had seen few or no white men. He carried the pipes with him, dressed in his Highland costume; and when stopping at forts, or wherever he found Indians, the bagpipes were put in requisition, much to the astonishment of the natives, who supposed him to be a relation of the Great Spirit, having, of course, never beheld so extraordinary a looking man, or such a musical instrument, which astonished them as much as the sound produced. One of the Indians asked him to intercede with the Great Spirit for him; but Frazer remarked, the petitioner little thought how limited his influence was in that quarter.

—*Paul Kane,* Wanderings of an Artist Among the Indians of North America, *c. 1845.*

DAVID JORDAN

"[Twelve Foot] Davis was the first to bring them the calicoes and tea and sugar and luxuries.

The first time Davis came he charged them nothing for all these things. Just treated them.

He married a nice Bear girl when she was 12 years old. She died at 17. They wanted to give him another girl—he said he didn't want one. He loved her too well."

—*Rev. John McDougall, Diary July 1909*

Interior detail of St. Bernard's Mission at Grouard. Bishop Emil Grouard painted the scene behind the altar.

He knew of an Indian at Ft. Liard, a Nahanni during McLeod's stay, who in a trance dreamt he saw Heaven and coming back described it—making a map of it. With one place barren and little good for hunting and others with places, valleys and rivers abounding in game.

—*Rev. John McDougall, Diary July 1909*

Chimney detail of the St. Jean Baptiste Mission near Falher.

DAVID JORDAN

Our houses were made of spruce logs mostly. We had only two windows in them, no upper floors, no glass, but a rawhide skin of a calf, deer or moose calf was used. Only the hair would be taken off. It was put on the window while wet, and nailed on with wooden pegs on slats around the window. When dry, it would be taut and might be used as a drum. It was not transparent, but gave light. Though not as good as glass, it had one advantage, no Peeping Tom was going to peep through your window. . . .

But before the house had been occupied two days, the owner had to invite the neighbors to a big dance. We danced reels, jigs and other old time dances. We had no tables; because we didn't have them we didn't miss them; no chairs or benches. We ate on the floor. A canvas was spread with a white cloth on top; then the set was ready for the meal. . . .

When the grain was very dry, we put it in the frying-pan adding a little grease, and when cooked brown, it was a good substitute for bread. We had no coffee, but again barley came to the rescue. We put the barley in the frying-pan, without hulling it, and when fried real black we used that for coffee. . . .

Metis from Lac Ste. Anne and St. Albert often visited each other, that is once or twice a year. These two settlements were of the same people, and they were related mostly. There would be a man or a family from Lac La Biche or Slave Lake who would come and live in the settlement. The two Settlements were all Catholics, L'Hirondelle, Belcourt, Gledus, Plante, Laderoute and Gauthier were of French descent. . . .

We used to see the Battle River people, off and on. Since they were Metis of French extraction like us, good fellowship prevailed, and some marriages took place. We did not come in contact with the Metis at Victoria; their being of Anglo-Saxon descent and of a different denomination, no visits, to my knowledge, were ever made to them.
—*Victoria Calihoo, "Early Life in Lac Ste. Anne and St. Albert in the 1870's,"* ALBERTA HISTORICAL REVIEW, *November 1953.*

GATEWAY TO THE NORTH

Edmonton was the main factor-house for the Saskatchewan District of the Hudson's Bay Co. and was the most important post in what was then Alberta.

Fur trade fort. Pioneer village. Klondike goldrush centre. Seat of government. Centre of learning. Oil capital of Canada. Edmonton has worn many cloaks since William Tomison established the first temporary trading post to bear the name in 1795.

As fur headquarters for decades, the fort and small community fell on hard times during the 1880 s when the transcontinental railroad was routed south through Calgary. When the steel ribbon finally found its way north in 1891, it did not cross the North Saskatchewan River — the new town of Strathcona boomed on the southern bank while Edmonton languished. (The key event in Edmonton's history may well have been the attempted clandestine relocation of the Land Titles Office to Strathcona. If outraged Edmontonians had not physically blocked the attempt, it is possible that "Strathcona" would be the major city of the north.)

Since the turn of the century, Edmonton has ridden the cycles of agriculture, land development and petroleum exploration. Construction, demolition, reconstruction follow each other in a dizzying spiral of constant activity. The city never sleeps.

Today's bustling urban centre still has a Hudson's Bay Company store near its centre, still receives and ships goods to the north, still prides itself as the most northerly of major North American cities.

The Gibson Block (commonly called the flat-iron building) was one of Edmonton's first office buildings, and still retains its distinctive charm.

The MacKay Avenue School. The name above the door was misspelled by a stonemason.

York boat on the Saskatchewan. As many as ten York boats were built each season at Fort Edmonton, and they carried loads of three tons plus eight crew members.

Bought a horse from an Indian, for 1 1/2 gal. of mixture, a blanket, & tobacco. At night late bothered by another who came into our bedroom screwed, & wanted to sell his horse. But we were obdurate, & very sulky so that he perceived it & asked if I wanted to fight with him. He was very good-humoured & jocose although pertinacious; we told him it was too late that night, but we would give him some in the morning. He said "you are very foolish for now I am drunk I don't care for my horse, but in the morning I shall be sober & shall be very fond of it." We said Keyarki; & he, finding it no go, left us.

Tuesday, May 26th.—In morning Indian brought his horse & we bought him for same price as the last; another came, but we could not trade, the liquor being finished. The last we bought a very good strong one. In afternoon we went across river to wash gold. Hardisty and Baptiste accompanied us; worked away at our tin pans, obtaining a perceptible quantity each time. They called us to supper, but forgot to send barge, & we had to wait an hour before we could make any one hear. After tried to collect our gold dust with mercury, but owing to stupidity in using tin dishes, & bad manipulation we lost it all.
—From Dr. Cheadle's Journal of his trip across Canada, 1863.

Monday, May 25th.—3 women & 6 children suffering from secondary syphilis! The Fort will be in a nice state eventually, I expect.

Aug. 14—Prayers twice, taught Lord's Prayer & Creed.

Aug. 15—A day of horror! Also what a contrast to the former scenes. Two murders committed in the morning near my tent, father & son shot dead by two half-caste. What a shock to my feelings to be near such awful scenes. It arose from a dispute respecting gambling. The elder of the two was the son of a Canadian & an Indian woman. He came, in the morning, near the tents of the murderers, carrying an axe. His son was with him bearing a gun which I learnt afterwards was not loaded. The father was shot through the head whilst scuffling with an Indian for the axe & the son almost at the same moment was shot thro' the breast. The former never spoke afterwards but the latter ran a few paces towards the tent saying only . . . "They have killed me." I buried them in one grave & pitched off from the scene of blood! In the evg. I talked on the awful event. When will these things cease?

The deceased was one whom the R.C. Priest had succeeded in beguiling away from me & he did not attend my services. He came, however, twice into my tent; at his last visit (the Sunday night before his death), I spoke to him on the subj. of brotherly love. I was asleep at the time of the occurence as were all in my tent. I could get but little rest in the night being so troubled by the poor starving dogs.
—*From the Journal of Robert T. Rundle, 1843.*

DAVID STERNTHAL.

Detail of tower at Fort Edmonton Park.

On the night of our arrival at Edmonton, the wind increased to a perfect hurricane, and we had reason to be thankful to Providence for our timely escape from the awful scene we now witnessed from our present place of safety, for, had we been one day later, we might have been involved in its fiery embrace. The scene on which our attention was now riveted, was the conflagration of the prairie through which we had passed but a few hours before. The scene was terrific in the extreme; the night being intensely dark gave increased effect to the brilliancy of the flames. We were apprehensive at one time of its crossing the river to the side on which the fort is situated, which must in that case have been destroyed. Our fears, too, for Mr. Rundell, whom we had left behind with the boys, were only relieved three days afterwards, when he arrived in safety. It appeared that he had noticed the fire at a long distance off, and immediately started for the nearest bend in the river, which with great exertions he reached in time, and succeeded in crossing. The mode resorted to by the Indians, when in the immediate vicinity of a prairie fire, is to set fire to a long patch in front of them, which they follow up, and thus depriving the fire in the rear of fuel, escape all but the smoke, which, however, nearly suffocates them.
—*Paul Kane, from* WANDERINGS OF AN ARTIST AMONG THE INDIANS OF NORTH AMERICA.

47

The prestigious Ravina Apartments retain the grandeur of another era.

DALE JARHAUS

DALE JARHAUS

DALE JARHAUS

The Hunter residence, in the Riverdale neighbourhood. Built by Edmonton pioneer, politician and entrepreneur Frank Oliver, the house is still occupied by the family of the original purchaser.

DALE JARHAUS

DALE JARHAUS

PROSPECTIVE IMMIGRANTS FROM IOWA

James Reilly, of Calgary, arrived from Des Moines, Iowa, on Monday's train, accompanied by Messrs. Fox and Dietz, delegates from Iowa, who are prospecting the North-West under Mr. Reilly's supervision. Both gentlemen are much pleased with the country, especially from the Lone Pine to Edmonton. They drove out to St. Albert on Tuesday and were very favorably impressed with the appearance of the harvest fields there and the samples of grain.

Iowa is a very prosperous and wealthy state, where the land is valued at from $50 an acre and upwards and where a large part of the farming population occupy rented land. They would gladly exchange their condition of renters for that of owners, but cannot purchase at the high price, and therefore many are desirous of removing to a region where good and cheap land can be had. Formerly the overflow went to Nebraska, Kansas or Dakota. These states have become discredited through bad seasons, and people are now more willing to try the, to them, unknown North-West rather than the proven failures of these other states. Co-operative dairying or the creamery system has reached a high pitch of profitable perfection in Iowa, and as this is a branch of agricultural industry for which Alberta is peculiarly adapted.

—EDMONTON BULLETIN, *Sept. 22, 1892*

Aug. 26, 1884

. . . the Dear Love wanted me by her all the time and I stayed by her head all day and tried to comfort her. tis my opinion the children would have been both born before twelve had poor Lillie not been so much swolen on the surface of her body. the pains came quick and strong and she had so much strength she put her arms around my neck every time I *never* thought she had such strength she worked hard till half past three when the first one was born. A fine little boy Dear Lillie was so much pleased that it was a boy. She saw the Dear little thing. when the Doctor took it out of the room she said Doctor put it somewhere where it won't get hurt. She was not too tired I was so glad she seemed so well. the doctor came back and found there was another when Lillie seemed to give up and think it was too much for her. We encouraged her in every way we could and she worked hard and patient for three hours when her strength entirely gave out when pains would come and she would try and say no good, no good then she begged the doctor to do something the child was nearly born the doctor could do nothing but give chloroform and take the instrument which he used in a very few minutes when another little boy was born dead. I held her hands and talked to her all the time she was quite sensible and knew everything but kept getting weaker all the time for about half an hour after the last one was born my Dear Love just stretched out her neck and quit breathing. I thought she fainted but no the truth was too plain. My Love was gone to Jesus her dear arms would never go around my neck anymore. I could not understand it I felt like I was in a dream I sat by her and held her hand waiting for her to open her eyes but she did not. they tied up her head and fixed her after the fashion of the dead. It is just a week since the funeral and it seems such a long time.

—*From the diary of James Henry Long of Namao.*

The First Presbyterian Church of Edmonton is dwarfed by its modern corporate neighbour.

The St. Josaphat Ukrainian Catholic Church celebrates a tradition of faith that is centuries old.

Friday Aug 29th [1879]

My Dear Dear Mother

  The mail just got in today and brought me 2 letters, one from you written July 13th and one from Charles Henry written July 1st. I was so glad to get them and hear you are all well at home. It was such a long time to wait for to get a letter, but after this I hope you will write so I will be able to get letters from you every mail. . . . I would give anything to see you, we would have such a good talk. If you could only come and see me, it would be so nice. I never was so happy in my life as I am now, but I often feel so lonely to see you, but Johnnie says he will let me go home in a year and a half more. He is the best fellow in the world. I have *never never* been sorry for marrying him. He would do anything for me. He felt so bad today when he read your letter.

[unsigned]

[P.S.]Please send me the receipt for wine, any kind will do. I think I will make some of cranberries.

—*Letter from Lovisa McDougall, wife of independent Edmonton merchant J.A. McDougall.*

The Season's Outstanding Event

PERSONAL VISIT OF

SIR JOHN

MARTIN HARVEY

MISS N. DE SILVA
and London Cast and Production

WEEK OF MARCH 28th

MONDAY, TUESDAY,
WEDNESDAY EVENINGS
(Matinee Wednesday)

"THE KING'S MESSENGER"

Frederick Jackson's Thrilling and
Engrossing Mystery Play

THURSDAY, FRIDAY, SATURDAY EVENINGS
(Saturday Matinee)

"THE BELLS"

The Great Drama of Crime and Haunting Remorse

EMPIRE THEATRE

MAIL ORDERS NOW RECEIVED

PRICES:

Evenings: 50c, 75c, $1.00, $1.50 and $2.00

Matinees: 50c, 75c, $1.00, Plus Tax

A.W. CAMERON, proprietor of the Empire Theatre, began operations on a new theatre today. The site is west of the Hudson's Bay corner on Jasper Avenue....The theatre will be opened on October 11 and 12th by a specially enlarged company.
—EDMONTON BULLETIN, *20 September 1906.*

EDMONTON CHOSEN AS THE CAPITAL
Beat Calgary out by Eight Votes
Mr. Simmons Voted for Calgary

Edmonton, April 26.—Edmonton gets the capital by a vote of sixteen for to eight against. Cardston, Lethbridge, Macleod, High River, Calgary, Gleichen, Red Deer and Rosebud voted for Calgary.
—*From the* LETHBRIDGE HERALD, *Thursday, 26 April 1906.*

EDMONTON POPULATION INCREASES TO 263

The unofficial census which has just been completed gives the following as the adult population of the principal settlements in this district, with the increase or decrease since the last census was taken in '78.

Edmonton settlement 263, increase 115.
Fort Saskatchewan 60, increase 1.
St. Albert 292, increase 114.
Lac Ste. Anne 30, decrease 28.
Lac La Biche 75, decrease 27.
Victoria 46, decrease 12.
Total 766. Total increase 163.

The apparent decrease in some of the settlements is on account of many who formerly were counted as half breeds taking the treaty, thereby taking rank as Indians. The total population has of course increased much more than is apparent, as children are not counted in this census.
—*From the* EDMONTON BULLETIN, *31 January 1881.*

St. Stephen's College on the University of Alberta campus. The building houses Alberta Culture's Historic Sites Service.

HOSE

The Strathcona Fire Hall, now home of the Walterdale Theatre.

Awning detail of the Strathcona Hotel.

Bard House (still owned by the Bard family).

On the city's south side, Old Strathcona preserves many of Edmonton's architectural landmarks. The arrival of the railroad to Strathcona in 1891 spurred a building boom along Whyte Avenue.

Edmonton Bulletin.

VOL. VI. EDMONTON, ALBERTA, SATURDAY, JULY 18TH, 1885. No. 38.

TELEGRAPHIC.

WINNIPEG, July 14, 1885.

No important foreign despatches.

Big Bear and several others are now on the way to Regina from Prince Albert.

Scouts have traced Little Poplar and band from near Battleford, and report him on the way to the boundary.

Gen. Brackenbury telegraphs from Fatniah, Egypt, that a letter which was received there on the 10th inst. states El Mahdi is dead.

No word has yet been received from the troops since they left Prince Albert. They are expected to reach Selkirk to-day or to-morrow.

Riel's counsel have arrived. They are F. X. Lemieux, M.P.P., Charles Fitzpatrick and J. W. Greenshields. All will appear at the opening of the trial on the 20th.

Poundmaker and twenty-two other prisoners from Battleford have arrived at Regina. Of this number ten men were sentenced at Battleford and are being brought to Stoney mountain.

Orange and green riots took place at Waterford, Belfast and a few places in England on Sunday, 12th inst. At Waterford several civilians were stabbed to death by soldiers. The populace became furious and many soldiers were maltreated.

WINNIPEG, July 17, 1885.

Big Bear, Whitecap and other Indian prisoners are at Qu'Appelle on their way to Regina.

Yesterday the House of Commons passed the act for the administration of justice in the North-West territories, including the clause prohibiting the carrying of improved fire arms except by permission of the lieutenant-governor. Sir John explained that the act would apply only in proclaimed districts. He said that in many districts people were inclined to be rebellious and could not be trusted with rifles.

Winnipeg has been in a fearful buzz of excitement over the return of the volunteers. Middleton's forces reached Selkirk on Wednesday morning. The 65th and Midland battalions went on home from that point. The Queen's Own and Grenadiers and Ottawa Footguards came in here with the general. The citizens were profoundly excited and the reception to the 90th was of the warmest character. A flattering address was presented to Gen. Middleton on behalf of the citizens. The field battery arrived last night and was received with similar greetings. All the eastern troops have gone home except the Queen's Own, Grenadiers, and York and Simcoe battalions, which are here, and the London battalion, which will arrive here to-morrow. The review will take place to-day and the grand procession to-night.

PRINCE ALBERT, July 15, 1885.

The battery was here on Saturday last.

The police are still engaged removing the stockade around the Presbyterian church.

The half-breed commission is now sitting here, and scrip being bought as fast as issued.

Mr. and Mrs. Gilbert Carter, and Mrs. Stackhouse started yesterday for a trip to Ontario.

STRAUBENZIE, July 14, 1885.

Steamer Northcote left Pitt for Edmonton yesterday morning.

Col. Smith is seriously ill at Pitt, and unable to leave his bed.

Forty-nine Cree Indians, with families, 236 in all, surrendered and gave up their arms to Col. Smith at Pitt on Saturday.

They are now camped there and being fed. Another band of 200 Crees is expected to ... surrender to-morrow.

... out and many

LOCAL.

RIVER very high, with some driftwood.

MAIL arrived on Tuesday evening, on time.

SHOWERY weather on Wednesday and Thursday.

No service in the Methodist church to-morrow.

CHOKE cherries and Saskatoon berries are plentiful.

R. MCRAE left for Calgary and the east on Tuesday.

F. D. WILSON arrived at Prince Albert on Thursday.

J. MOWAT arrived from Calgary with freight on Wednesday last.

REV. A. ROBERTSON and Mr. Gough left for Calgary on Tuesday last.

SCHOOL closed on Wednesday for the summer holidays, which will probably be about five weeks.

STAGE left on Friday morning. Passengers: Mrs. Jas. Goodridge and two children, and Frank Osborne.

THE North-West is expected to arrive from Grand Rapids about the 26th inst. with a cargo of general freight.

W. R. BRERETON is in charge of a gang of men improving the road to the Athabasca landing for the H. B. Co.

CAPT. MACKINTOSH, of No. 7 company, is commandant of the military post here since the departure of Col. Ouimet.

E. CAREY, of Norris & Carey, C. Fraser, and Mrs. T. Hourston left for Winnipeg on Wednesday by way of Calgary.

ALEX. TAYLOR, telegraph operator, has received a number of North-West ordinances of 1884 for sale at 60 cts apiece.

THE post-office notice that mails arriving after five p. m. would not be distributed the same evening has been rescinded.

TRADE commissioner Wrigley, and chief factor Hardisty of the H.B.Co., are expected to arrive from Calgary next week.

MR. AND Mrs. Youmans, of Whitefish lake, arrived from Victoria on Saturday last, and went on to Calgary on Wednesday.

HARDISTY & Fraser's mill is gristing at present on last year's crop. About 1,300 bushels of wheat are now in the mill.

A. ADAMSON, of Clover Bar, left for Calgary this morning per M. McCauley's team. He is bound for Ontario to purchase stock.

MRS. JAS. GOODRIDGE fell from her buggy near Norris & Carey's store on Thursday afternoon, receiving several severe bruises.

IT is rumored that a band of horses which was driven in to Edmonton two weeks ago, from Bow river, had some stolen animals in it.

A FREIGHTING outfit belonging to P. McCallum and W. Taylor arrived on the south side on Friday evening, loaded for Norris & Carey,

NEW potatoes for dinner was the way many of the Edmonton people celebrated the 12th of July. Pretty early for 53½ degrees north latitude.

THE temporary stockade erected along the river front of the H. B. fort during the Indian excitement by the Edmonton volunteers has been taken down.

THE new mining scow is being rapidly constructed at the point below Hardisty & Fraser's mill, but the high water may possibly stop operations on her.

SOME of the returned transport horses which were shot, on account of being disabled, on the flat below the fort last week were not properly buried, and now cause a very unpleasant stench.

... more teams of the transport train, ... straggled in from Pitt on ... The last of them

SHOULD the Indians make another break here the settlers will be in a better fix to receive them. There are 250 Snider Enfields and 80 45-75 Winchesters in the government stores, with an unlimited amount of ammunition dated 1884.

T. GREAVES arrived from Calgary on Thursday with a wagon a cart train of freight. At the Black Mud he lost a horse, which broke its picket line and strayed away. He searched a day, but was unable to find it. The animal belonged to W. H. Carson,

THE money taken from the territorial funds in 1883 to pay the idemnity of members of the North-West Council for the session of that year is being refunded by the federal government, the amount, $2,400, appearing in the supplementary estimates.

A SEIZURE of beer in Smith & Hurley's was made during the week and held for analysis to prove whether it contained an intoxicating principle or not. The beverage dignified by the name of beer in the North West is not supposed to be intoxicating, though it sometimes is.

AMONGST the benefits flowing from the rebellion may be reckoned the vast improvement in manner and matter of the Prince Albert Times since its resurrection. It displays vigorous ability and a dsire to tell the whole truth, which it is to be regretted it did not evince before.

D. M. MCDOUGALL arrived on Wednesday with a band of 75 cattle and and six horses for sale. The animals are from O. S. Main's herd at the mouth of Little Bow river, and are in splendid condition for beef. They came through the winter with slight loss. Cattle are dear in the range country.

A BUCKBOARD belonging to Dr. Wilson, which had been left at Sanderson & Looby's blacksmith shop for repairs, disappeared on Friday night of last week. It was discovered on Saturday, cached in a bluff near a teamsters' camp in rear of Drunken lake. The teamsters disclaimed all knowledge of how it got there. No arrests.

The Calgary Herald has found out that the reason arms were not issued to the Edmonton home guard by Col. Ouimet was that the men would not take the oath of allegiance, and says. "This little circumstance was not mentioned in the BULLETIN." The reason the circumstance was not mentioned in the BULLETIN was that it did not occur.

IT is said that a teamster of the transport train, on his way back from Pitt, coolly loaded up the mower and seeder belonging to the Indian farm at Saddle lake, and took them through to Calgary with him. Also that another took an I. D. wagon from Pitt, while the horse ridden by Ma-ma-nook, the Indian killed at Pitt, a fine black stallion, which was made a prize by the scouts, was taken from them and claimed by McLean, who asserted that he was the lawful owner.

PITT was always an excellent fur trading post, and last winter it does not seem to have been an exception judging from the piles of fur found scattered around the Indian camps near by. Some of the teamsters made a good haul in beaver, and could have made a better on lynx had they known its value. Lynx skins were more numerous than any other kind and were being bought, sold and traded amongst the men at from 15c to 60c apiece, while their actual value is $2.

AN elaborately gotten up circular from Pinkerton's detective agency arrived at the Edmonton post-office this mail. The circular has a fine lithograph of one Richard Seaman Scott, who, it appears was lately paying teller of the Manhattan bank, New York, and succeeded in getting away with the bank to the amount of $100,000. A reward of $5,000 is offered for the handing over of Mr. Scott to the New York authorities. The circular is dated June 5th. Mr. Scott is probably in ... is not likely to be at Edmonton. ... to Beaver river ...

THE prompt manner in which the government indebtedness incurred by the Alberta field force at Edmonton has been paid off is worthy of all praise. With the exception of a hitch for about a week every account has been paid through the H.B.Co. in cash or by cash draft as soon as approved. This action has almost paralyzed the business community with surprise. It was expected that in accordance with long established custom months or years would elapse before the suniah would be forthcoming. If the same promptitude had always been exercised there would not have been so much dissatisfaction. But it is never too late to mend.

GEN. STRANGE'S coolness in the fight at Stand Off coulee near Pitt was remarked by all. He accompanied the advance of the 65th and Light Infantry into the valley and stood exposed to the fire of the Indians trying to make out their movements. The bullets were flying pretty thickly and at last one went through the general's trousers. He stooped down took the cloth between his finger and thumb, fixed his eye-glass and examined the hole. "Ha, Haa! Dial (Major Dale), I believe they're sheuting at me," he remarked, whereupon he mounted his horse, and rode along to another part of the field, surveying the Indian position all the while.

THE supply of deer in the Athabasca district is a failure this year, and the deficiency has to be made up by flour and bacon from Edmonton. It is an ill wind that blows nobody good. The freight is to be sent out immediately. The scarcity of deer extended to the Mackenzie river district. The people are not suffering from want of food, but the trade of deer meat at the H.B. forts has been so small that they have no supplies on hand with which to provision their boats' crews on the annual trip for the trading outfit. The robbery of the stores at Green lake and Isle la Crosse has, of course, made matters worse in the case of freight going in by the Long Portage route, of which a large quantity is on the way.

NEW ADVERTISEMENTS.

KELLY'S RESTAURANT.—In rear of saloon. Meals at all hours. Best table in town.

LOST — $5.00 REWARD. — At noon on Tuesday the 14th inst., near Black Mud creek on the Calgary trail, a large, light grey Canadian horse, about 16 hands high, eleven years old, heavy fore-top and tail, was shod only on front feet, and had leather halter on. No brand, but had marks of scalds on both sides. Finder is requested to leave the animal at Sanderson & Looby's blacksmith shop, or with the undersigned, when he will receive the above reward. W. H. CARSON, Sturgeon river.

NORTH-WEST MOUNTED POLICE.

TENDERS

For the following supplies to be delivered at the Mounted Police

BARRACKS, FORT SASKATCHEWAN,

Will be received by the undersigned up to

NOON, ON THE 31ST DAY OF JULY, 1885.

HAY, (upland) to be cut in August and delivered, one quarter during August and balance during September and October — 200 tons.

CORDWOOD, Dry, to be delivered during September and following months as required — 200 cords.

The person to whom the contract is awarded ... to furnish satisfactory ... formal contract

The Edmonton Bulletin, *actual size. Frank Oliver's weekly was the first newspaper published in Alberta.*

THE natural increased demand for *Coca-Cola* has made it necessary for us to open factories throughout the West.

The enormous sale of *Coca-Cola* in Canada has grown by reason of its appeal to thirsty palates and its purity and goodness.

Coca-Cola has a place in every home. It is a delicious and refreshing beverage which millions of people consider the best. Suitable for any company, any time, any place.

Coca-Cola in bottles is obtainable everywhere. Buy it by the case from your dealer.

is now bottled in your locality

New *Coca-Cola* bottling factories have been opened at the following Western points:

WINNIPEG,
Manitoba

BRANDON,
Manitoba

SASKATOON,
Saskatchewan

MOOSE JAW,
Saskatchewan

REGINA,
Saskatchewan

EDMONTON,
Alberta

CALGARY,
Alberta

LETHBRIDGE,
Alberta

VANCOUVER,
British Columbia

REMEMBER the times last summer, and the summer before, when the weather was hot and sultry.

There was summerfallowing to be done, roads to grade, fences to repair and plenty of other work to be done. BUT you probably also remember the dust, hot wind and sun.

Remember how much you would have appreciated a cool sparkling drink of some thirst quenching beverage? *Coca-Cola* would have been just the right drink then, and it will give you satisfaction this summer, too, if you remember when in town to ask your dealer for it—by the case.

As settlement spread over Alberta, so did the trappings of civilization. This Coca-Cola pamphlet dates from the 1920s.

The LeMarchand Mansion. When built, it was Edmonton's poshest apartment.

Constructed in 1898-99, St. Joachim's Catholic Church dates its beginnings to 1854, when the first Catholic mission was established at Fort Edmonton.

The Magrath Mansion is one of the most splendid homes ever built in Edmonton.

DALE JARHAUS

Friday Oct. 18, 1912

Mother's Bridge was a great success. Mrs. Dickens won first prize, a crochet collar that Bea made and Mrs. MacDonald won second an embroidery bag. The tea afterwards was very nice too I think. Mrs. Mowat poured coffee, and Mrs. Emery tea. Mrs. Hislop served the ices and Alice McKenny, Gwen Barnes, Jean Dawson and Isabel Paxton helped Beatrice and me serve. We went to a dance tonight too. Dyson Phelps took me and Mr. Carter took Bea. I had an awfully good time, danced with Dr. Mills and Gerald Paxton and heaps of others.

—Diary of Marjorie Mc.V. Saunders.

The impressive colonnade of the LeMarchand Mansion.

DALE JARHAUS

Xmas was a quiet day with us, the usual routine, only an extra dinner. No fowl of course, only roast beef. Xmas Eve Mr. McGilvery came in from Victoria, he is our visiter until after New Years. Xmas night I had Mr. Sinclair, our Land lord, for tea. He came up with Mr. Mc. After tea Mr. Little berry came to spend the evening. Mr. Sinclair & Mr. McGilvery went down to t[he] Fort to spend the evening with Colonel Stuart. Our first door neighbour, Colin Fraisher, had a dance, so George Gouler our Man went. We had great fun getting him ready to go. Johnnie lent him a white collar & George his neckties & I put some scent on his hankerchief, & I tell you he thought he was rigged out. Johnnie went over about 10 o'clock to see what was going on & they was hoeing the red river gig & clog dances right down. The girls had on red and plain dresses & lots of red ribbons. He said the babies was rolling around in every direction. The bed was piled up full near the celling & some mischievus person changed the shawls on them so the wemon did not know their own young one. He said they had a big brass kettle setting on the coals full of beef, & the tea in a dirty old boiler. They had potatoes & plum pudding, cakes, & I tell you it takes the half breeds to enjoy them selves, and the white people goes to.

—*Letter from Lovisa McDougall to her brother, describing Christmas, 1879 at Fort Edmonton.*

June 11, 1925

His Worship Mayor Blatchford
and Commissioner Mitchell
City of Edmonton
Gentlemen,

The Edmonton Tree Planting Committee wish to express their appreciation of the grant of $200.00 received from the City towards their funds.

We have this season brought into the City and planted on the boulevards and Public grounds 1,500 native birch; sold on the market at cost a car load of trees and shrubs, given lectures on City Beautifying and Tree Planting to over 5,000 children, and eleven lectures to community leagues and other meetings, distributed thousands of pamphlets and circulars educating the citizens in planting of trees and care of same.

With the cooperation and support of the City, the Merchants and the Citizens, the Committee has been enabled to do much to make a better and more beautiful Edmonton.

Yours respectfully,
The Tree Planting Committee

I attended the convention of Women's Institutes in Edmonton and had a *very* pleasant time. It was well done, good music, all the bigwigs, and Gov. to help, and very, very different to our own higgledy-piggledy affair in Calgary, but their line of work to tell you the truth does not interest me very much—there is too much of the housekeeping business about it, and for my part I think the farm women want to be taken out of their housekeeping troubles, and made to realize there are other things of interest in the world, and that they do their housekeeping all the better for thinking of outside affairs.
—*Irene Parlby*
Letter to Violet McNaughton
March 14, 1916
Irene Parlby was a leader in Canada's suffrage movement.

Suffragette songsheet from 1920. Albertans Emily Murphy, Irene Parlby, Violet McNaughton, Louise McKinney and Nellie McClung were the driving force behind securing citizens' rights for women in Canada.

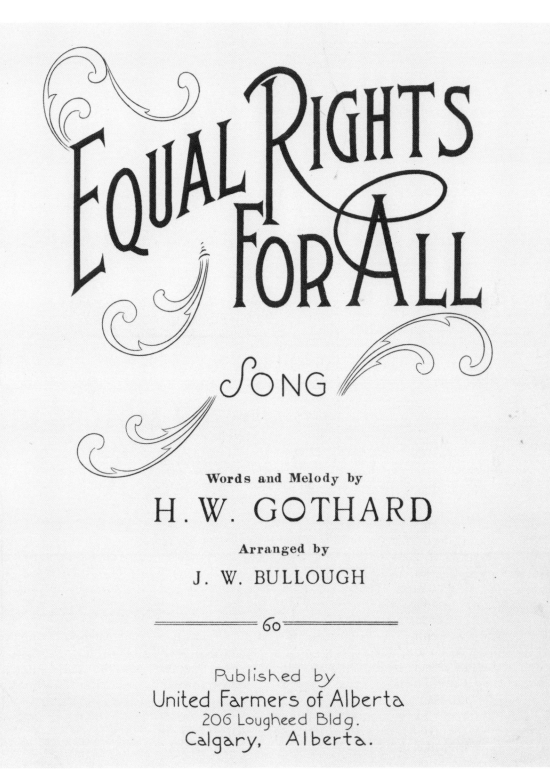

EQUAL RIGHTS FOR ALL

SONG

Words and Melody by

H. W. GOTHARD

Arranged by

J. W. BULLOUGH

60

Published by

United Farmers of Alberta
206 Lougheed Bldg.
Calgary, Alberta.

HALLOWED HILLS AND SHINING MOUNTAINS

"Behold the shining mountains!" wrote Anthony Henday in his journal. It was the record of his first glimpse of the Rocky Mountains. The snow-capped peaks beckoned across the foothills, urging the weary traveller to break from the monotony of the prairies. Their cool beauty continues to lure the adventurous from around the world. Jasper, Banff, Lake Louise, Waterton Lakes, the Columbia Icefields — these scenic marvels along Alberta's western border are perhaps the province's best-known and best-loved locales.

If the agricultural production and energy resources of the plains, parkland and the north are the lifeblood of the Alberta economy, the foothills and Rockies are what quicken the heart. It is little wonder that David Thompson chose the site for Rocky Mountain House at the edge of the Kootenay

The breathtaking slopes of the Rockies and the crest of the Continental Divide. BONNIE BENTLEY

Plain. The first ranchers in western Canada worked hard to keep their stock, but had the serendipitous fortune to drive their cattle among the ridge-backed foothills in the Rockies' great shadow. The exalted scenery has moved the pens of poets, from Stephan Stephansson to Sid Marty.

The riches are not only scenic. Coal in the Crowsnest. Hydroelectricity in the Kananaskis. Oil and gas from Turner Valley to Nordegg. But these material assets are secondary; for Albertans, the real worth of the mountains is as an anchor for the spirit.

The old mine entrance at Cadomin, on the east slopes of the Rocky Mountains just south of Hinton.

The front cover of an Australian brochure advertises the lure of the Canadian Rockies in the 1920s.

The CANADIAN ROCKIES

TICKETS, BERTHS AND FURTHER INFORMATION

FROM THOS. COOK & SON

269 Collins Street

MELBOURNE

Cook's Travellers' Cheques - Good Everywhere

From a New Neighborhood

From its source in the rugged Rockies
The Red Deer river flows,
'Twixt hollows, hills and valleys
O'er Alberta's eastern slopes.

Herders inhabit wherever,
Herds are all over the fold
Scattered, and some are wethers,
Some bulls both vicious and bold.

Here Satan's serfs are retired
And the Gods forsaken are freed,
Like by Lethe the Greeks groped uninspired
The decalogue was a forgotten creed.

—Stephan G. Stephansson, from ANDVÖKUR.
Translated by Helgi Hornford.

Jack of All Trades

I, mostly my own doctor,
A lawyer and builder smart,
A teacher, prince and pastor,
A horse, a plow and cart.

—Stephan G. Stephansson, from ANDVÖKUR.
Translated by Sigurdur Wopnford.

A homesteader near Red Deer from 1889 until his death in 1927, Stephan G. Stephansson is acclaimed as Iceland's greatest poet since the 13th century.

Detail of Stephansson House.

DAVID STERNTHAL

Stephansson House at Markerville, southeast of Red Deer. From his study window, Stephan Stephansson could view the distant mountains.

Plovers in a Field

You've gathered to feed on my grain here;
I bid you a welcome, eat hearty and free,
For you are the guests I have longed for,
Like plovers in Iceland so precious to me.
Pick only the choicest of kernels,
My holding is small, and meagre the fare,
But guests which have come such a distance
Deserve all the best that is there.

No doubt you bring news of the springtime,
Your flights over meadows and blossoming
   tree,
How blithesome the young in their winging
High over the land and the sea.
But suddenly something forgotten,
Illumines my mind with a scene,
Like flowers adorning a grave-mound,
Or glimpses of loves that have been.

But no, you just feed there in silence,
—'Twas only a vision from past summer
   days—
Not one of you bursts into singing!
In Iceland's cool autumn you sang me your
   lays,
And is not the spring here less cruel,
The weather here warmer and richer the land,
The grass in the meadows here greener,
And Nature's a generous hand?

I know now—tho slow to discern it—
The art of your singing is tuned with the land,
Creations from lava and glacier
Are the themes of your greatest command.
So like when the storm of the ocean
Is thundering poetry strong,
We sing when the sorrows assail us
But pleasures can rob us of song.

—*Stephan G. Stephansson, from* ANDVÖKUR.
Translated by Paul Sigurdson.

McDougall United Church near Morley.

DAVID STERNTHAL

69

Ottawa 17th Dec 1880

The Right Hon'ble Sir John A. MacDonald
Minister of the Interior
Sir

I have for some time past been making arrangements to establish a Stock Farm in the North West, with the view of affording emigrants settling in that part of the Dominion an opportunity of stocking their farms with improved breeds of Cattle and Horses, and also in the belief that a large foreign trade can be developed in the Export of stock from the Canadian North West.

At the present time settlers going into the new territory are compelled either to transport their stock from Ontario, at an expense usually in excess of their means, or they are forced to purchase inferior animals at high prices from the United States.

Owing to the limited number of domestic cattle in the country the government have in the past been obliged to purchase the cattle and beef supply for the police-force and for the Indians from Montana Territory. The amount thus paid to foreigners for food supplies has been very considerable.

Now as we have ample grazing grounds on the north side of the line, it is obviously in the interest of the Dominion to favour in every legitimate manner an industry that will enable the Government to purchase food supplies within its own border and allow settlers an opportunity of purchasing improved stock in the country.

In order to render the enterprise fairly remunerative and permit sales commencing within two or three years to be made, a large capital has to be invested, I propose starting with a herd of from two to three thousand animals including about seventy five thoroughbred bulls which must be imported from England. This will involve an expenditure of about $125,000.

To warrant so large an outlay, I should like to feel confident of obtaining the Lease of a sufficient area to enable me to increase the Herd to 10,000 animals and the right to purchase a sufficient acreage within the leased area for a farm on which to erect the necessary buildings for a certain amount of winter protection and forage—as I deem it prudent in testing what is largely an experiment to be provided with both food and stabling in case of an unusually severe winter.

The *thirty fifth* Section of "The Dominion Land Act 1879" authorizes the Governor in Council to grant Leases of unoccupied Dominion lands for grazing purposes.

The section of country I have selected may be described as being bounded on *the east* by the 114 parallel, on *the south* by the southern branch of High River which flows east into Bow River, on *the west* by The Rocky Mountains, and on *the north* by a line twenty miles north of the 51st degree of latitude and parallel with it, shown within the red lines on the accompanying section of the North West plan. Excluding of course the land immediately around Calgary and also the Indian Reserve at Morleyville.

This area is 150 Miles from the Railway lines, and is unoccupied.

From the best information available I do not think that it has any special attractions for settlers who desire to farm as there are vast areas to the east of it that will for many years be more desirable for settlers whose object is to carry on general farming.

To enable me to commence operations during the coming spring it will be incumbent on me to make immediate arrangements. I should therefore feel obliged if you would favour me by an early reply to this application.
I have the honour
to be your obedient Servant
M.H. Cochrane
—Senator M.H. Cochrane established the first ranch in Western Canada, near the town that bears his name.

There was never any notice given as to land about Calgary being reserved as far as I know. When I settled in 1875 the police tried to prevent me cutting wood on my own claim, for my own use, and put up notices that they claimed all the wood and grass for ten miles around Calgary. I have known of my own personal knowledge some forty or fifty settlers being driven out of the country because they could not get land, and just now a number of young men from near Chicago have been searching to find land to settle on, and cannot as it is all taken up by settlers, leases or reserves of some kind. I had about a year ago a number of cattle on the Cochrane range. There was not an animal on the range belonging to the company and the manager drove my cattle off onto burnt ground. I compelled him to drive them back but lost 35 head of my cattle through the action of the company. Unless the country is

DAVID STERNTHAL.

The bronze monument at the Cochrane Ranche site faces west towards the Rockies.

opened up at once for settlement and patents granted to those entitled to them I would as soon as not burn up all my improvements and leave the country. For the present I defend my claim as my neighbours do, behind my Winchester. Unless the land is all opened up for homestead entry all must either fight for our rights or leave the country and if I am compelled to leave, I will leave marks on the trail behind me.
—*Sam Livingston, quoted in* CALGARY HERALD, *9 April 1885.*

"I remember so well the old Opera House where my sisters and I went to the silent movies. The serial, *The Moon Riders*, went on for years. We were always so happy when payday came. Our dad would bring home five cents' worth of candy for us and give each a nickel for the movies."
—*Anne Topak, from* THE CROWSNEST AND ITS PEOPLE

McDougall United Church, near Morley. Father and son missionaries George and John McDougall (along with trader David) were the first to cut a southern path from Edmonton toward Calgary in 1873.

The Colonel's Cabin in the heart of the Kananaskis.

DAVID STERNTHAL

We soon met the River Kananaskis, and crossed it. Here it was flowing in an easterly direction, but its course before reaching the Bow River is northerly. Our course to this point has been south by west, and our distance from the entry to the pass about six miles. We now had a magnificent view of the valley of the Kananaskis River, hemmed in on either side by an unbroken wall of mountains, the sides of which, for about 1,000 feet, are richly clad with pines. After a short halt for dinner, we followed up the course of the Kananaskis till 6 p.m., when we encamped for the night. If it were not for the density of the woods, and the obstructions caused by the fallen timber, there would be no great difficulty in taking carts as far as this point. Our Stone Indian hunter shot a black tail deer to-day.

—From John Palliser's Journals, 1858, describing the Kananaskis Valley very near the Colonel's cabin, which was the headquarters for a German PoW camp in World War II.

1906
Heather Brae Jan the 19th

Miss Jennie Magee
    Dear Sister

You will be surprised to hear from me after so many years. Well, I have sad news for you. My Dear little wife is dead and I am the Lonelyest man in all the world. She gave birth to little Daughter on the 27th of December. Three days after she went out of her mind and on the 7th of January she took Pneumonia and Died about half past three in the afternoon. We Buryed her tuesday afternoon in a little cemetary on the Prairy about 5 miles from here. I am writing to you to see if you will come and keep house for me and raise my little Baby. I would not like to influence you in any way as I am afraid you would be lonely. When I have to go from home as I will now and again you are used to so much stir in the city. I have 400 acres of land and I have 9 or ten cows and some hens. If you come you can make all you can out of the Butter and eggs and I might be able to pay you a small wage besides. Write to me and let me know as soon as possible what you think about the proposition. . . .

from your affectionate brother,
Wm Magee
Heather Brae, Alta

DAVID STERNTHAL

When a coal mine was started near Canmore in the early part of this century, the mine manager built his home in the idyllic shadow of the mountains.

The remnants of the International Coal and Cole mineworks near Coleman, in the Crowsnest Pass.

"The clothes were washed on the old faithful scrub board with plenty of home made laundry soap. . . . The miners' clothes and other grubbies took great pains. Beads of perspiration were seen on mother's brow as she scrubbed relentlessly and often blisters appeared on her hands."
—*Ethel Dobeck,* THE CROWNEST AND ITS PEOPLE

At a Distance... This is a land of mirages. The mountains are constantly changing colour and shape as they come and go in the mist....One could take numerous photographs of them but no two pictures would be identical....On a winter's morning, "with bright, clear air around each deathly white peak and darkness on the slopes," the mountains then appear as "a row of clear, white snowdrifts"....The mountain slopes to the west and south shimmer in their radiance, but the passes and hollows are flecked a shadowy blue in the midday sun....Or, towards the north, they appear in the morning mirage as a narrow, even steel blue belt with grey tinges and a hint of daylight above....To the extreme south and north, the mountains look like blue pillars, some are suspended, some resemble pyramids and others are shaped like hourglasses. Towards the north, the mountains are more diamond shaped, forever changing and running together in a kaleidoscope of shape and colour.

The Most Striking Mountain—Southwest from here is the strangest mountain, rising up with wide and low cols to the south. The north face is jagged while the south face is nearly perpendicular....I am very fond of this chap. It is called "Devil's Head," possibly from an Indian name....
—*Stephan G. Stephansson, Letter to Eggert Johannsson, 19 January 1908. Translated by Bjorgvin Sigurdson.*

At the back of Tunnel Mountain, and in the valley, is a big enclosure of 800 acres in which Buffalies, Caribou (deer) and angora sheep roam at will and multiply. We drove right among the Buffalies and snapshotted them without their taking any notice of us; but our driver said it would not be safe to get down and walk about among them. After leaving the "corral" we drove on to some hot Sulpher Springs and Baths, where there are good bath houses, where bathing dresses are provided and water together.
—*From the diary of Clara Southwell, Sept. 17, 1910*

Feb. 21, 1841
Sunday. Off at 8 o'clock. Full of thoughts of the Rocky Mts.; expected to see them this morning but was disappointed. The snow that was left on the ground was very soft & rendered travelling over it very fatiguing. I proceeded a long distance before the Mts. became visible, nor did they then excite in my mind those feelings which I had anticipated. How uncertain is everything here below! How long & ardently I had thought of them & how anxiously I had enquired when I should see them. But how different were the feelings to what I had anticipated. I was weary with travelling. It was Sunday. . . . I was also observing at this time a track of blood on the snow & I conjectured that the driver was treating the dogs unmercifully & at times thoughts of this banished all thoughts of the mountains, for that man must be a brute that can feel happy when misery is before him. The Mts. have at first, when seen from a distance, the appearance of clouds & the reflection of the sun beaming on their snowy summits gives them a very interesting appearance.
—*From the journal of the Reverend Robert Terrill Rundle, Wesleyan Missionary.*

April 3, 1885

67°F-33°F. Fine.

Dunlap went to Stand Off to get a few supplies and see Police. He came back early and reported that there is a very good chance of the indians breaking out. It was to be decided today or tomorrow whether they would or not. I drove into town to get some arms, as we were not prepared and took Barker along.

Kootenai started for home this morning and found a 2 year old heifer mired at Spring coulee and came back and I went up with him and pulled her out, and he came back with me. I found a big roan cow dead up there two. Fell down bank into creek.

April 4

72°F-34°F. Fine.

They are very anxious about the indians in town and have double guards on every night. I got two rifles and two carbines, and a lot of ammunition and came out. I just got home before an outfit of 15 or more indians came up from Stand Off, full gallop, and swung around through the horses for some time.

Dunlap went over to the camp on the Kootenai in the evening and left his winchester there.

The heifer we pulled out of the mire at Spring coulee cannot live.

T. Dunn and Milt Jones commenced work this morning.

April 5

72°F-39°F. Fine.

J. Smith came up. Dunlap and Dunn went down to try and pull out cow mired near Smiths. They could not get her to get up.

Killed 3 year old steer in P.M. Dressed about 550 lbs.

April 6

41°F-32°F. Dull and cold. Snow flurries.

Robertson started in harrowing. Smith hunting bulls. He thought he saw someone watching him or Brown's horses. Dunn hunting horses found 9 more near Chas. Craig's. Dunlap and Paton went to town. There were 3 indians poking around here today.

April 7

51°F-12°F. Fine.

Robertson sowed first bottom 5 1/4 acres.

Went to Pincher Creek in P.M. with Lize. Took supper at Halifax Ranch, and went to Col. Macleod's for the night.

Dunlap came back in the evening.

April 8

60°F-22°F. Fine.

I got home at 6 P.M. Had lunch at Geddes'.

Davy commenced work this morning.

Dunlap thinks the outlook for the indians making trouble is pretty serious.

Capt. Perry and others are sending their families east.

April 9

67°F-37°F. Fine but windy.

Robertson sowed half of the second piece of oats.

Davy and Jones on fence.

Const. Hilliard came up from Stand Off. He says the indians are quiet and busy at their work.

From the Cochrane Ranche diary.

On the morning of April 29, 1903, a massive rockslide slid from the face of Turtle Mountain and buried the town of Frank in the Crowsnest Pass. The debris stretches for miles along the valley.

DAVID CUNNINGHAM

Looking east from the top of the bluff at Head-Smashed-In Buffalo Jump. The multiple layers of bones at the base of the kill site bear testimony to the centuries of use by the Plains Indians.

July 11th, Sunday—We were visited by a body of about 70 of the Surcee tribe, headed by the chiefs richly attired in dresses ornamented with porcupines' quills, and trimmed with ermine. We invited them to sit down and smoke. The chiefs were pleased with their reception, and inquired all about the purposes of our journey; they remained with us the whole night. We observed that several had lost a joint of one of their fingers. This we learnt was the consequence of a custom common to them with many other kindred tribes, of biting off the joint of a finger when unsuccessful in the performance of a vow. Among their women also, as among those of the Blackfeet, it is not uncommon to find many without a nose, or minus an ear, bitten off by their husbands in a fit of jealousy.
—*John Palliser, 11 July 1858,* THE PALLISER PAPERS.

Blood Indian tepees.

The "Stoneys" were much disappointed when they heard from us that there are no buffalo for many days to the eastward, and were, therefore, off every day hunting along the river valleys for deer and bears. At nightfall on the 12th, a party of 19 hunters that had started in the morning were still absent, and the camp was much alarmed for their safety, as some one had seen fresh horse tracks, and it was also said strange Indians, at a few miles to the south. We therefore spent the first part of the night on the alert, but about two o'clock most of the hunters returned, loaded with elk and bears' meat. They had killed three grizzly bears, and one of the party had been wounded in the encounter, so that he had to remain behind with three of his companions to take care of him. They said he was not badly hurt, only very stiff and sore from his wounds.

I had a long talk with the chiefs about what was likely to become of them and the other Indian tribes. They said that every year they find it more difficult to keep from starving, and that even the buffalo cannot be depended upon as before, because being now only in large bands, when one tribe of Indians are hunting then the other tribes have to go without until the band migrates into their country. The Stoneys are all Christians, and some of them can read and write in their own language, using the Cree syllabic characters, which were invented by the Wesleyan missionaries. They are very desirous of having tools and a few simple agricultural implements; and, as they are very steady, I have no doubt that if they were supplied with these, and direction given to their efforts, the best part of them would soon settle down, and leave their vagrant mode of life. Their chiefs at least seem to be quite in earnest about the matter.

—*Dr. James Hector, a member of the Palliser Expedition, 12 August 1859, in* THE PALLISER PAPERS.

WHERE THE ELBOW MEETS THE BOW

When North-West Mounted Police Inspector E.A. Brisebois established Fort Calgary in 1875, the site had little to offer except fresh water and a strategic location. Within ten years, Calgary was Alberta's largest and most important centre. It remains the economic crossroads of Alberta.

Compared to Edmonton, with its long-standing fur trade tradition, Calgary was a mere upstart. But the transcontinental Canadian Pacific Railway went by a southern route, reaching Calgary in 1882. By the end of that decade, the shanty town had been transformed into a city with handsome sandstone buildings and a burgeoning population. The settlement of Alberta took on a new pattern.

Oil and cattle. These two cornerstones of Calgary's economy have become emblematic of the city. Since the first Stampede in 1912, Calgary has hosted the world's

Column detail of the Royal Bank, Calgary.

largest rodeo every July. Cattle shaped the image of Calgary, but settlement and farming in the surrounding region made it grow. The promise of the 1880s was fulfilled in the booming prosperity of the decade before World War I. To that period belong even the first major oil explorations, undertaken in the Turner Valley just to the south.

No wonder Calgary's first urban society dates to that period, linked by the railway to the splendours of the mountain wilderness nearby. Though the sandstone, brick and frame edifices of old Calgary form a contrast to the glass and steel skyscrapers of the modern petroleum era, the remaining vestiges recall the ambition and elegance of another energetic community.

CALGARY EYE OPENER

CALGARY, SATURDAY, MARCH 9, 1912

Calgary. March 20, '07

Premier Rutherford
Strathcona
Dear Mr. Rutherford,

Permit me to congratulate you on the splendid work accomplished by your government during the session just closed. Your wisdom in protecting the treasury from the bold onslaughts of that fake immigration association and your kindness towards the Canadian Alpine Club have gained for you the solid friendship of my little rag—if that friendship is worth anything.

By way of reciprocity I shall go out of my way to speak in favor of Strathcona as the proper place for the Provincial University. You will get it anyhow, but I may be of some use in dispelling any ill feeling that may arise down here when the final announcement is made.

Wishing you continued success in your high office, believe me

Yours very truly,
R.C. Edwards

—Letter from Bob Edwards, editor of Calgary's irreverent paper THE EYE OPENER.

Eye Openers

R. C. EDWARDS
Editor and Proprietor.

Phone 1730

Subscription $1 per year

Correspondents are requested to address us to P. O. Box 2090, Calgary.

The bona fide circulation of The Eye Opener is now **30,500.** We invite inspection of our books. The management (there is a management now) is arranging to turn this thing into an eight-page paper, as there are too many ads for the size of the sheet. This is the first time we have reached the 30,000 mark and the occasion is surely well worthy of a drunk.

The Chamber of Commerce building in Calgary reflects the city's fine tradition of sandstone facades.

Those green-eyed sumphs up at Edmonton killed the Calgary University bill by a vote of 17 to 15. Well, this makes things so much easier for us Conservatives down here at the next political election. We know where we are at now.

It will have to be Calgary College now instead of Calgary University, but once affiliated

Interior of the Chamber of Commerce building.

with the famous McGill University, students will be able to pass the regular McGill examinations and receive McGill degrees. This should place Calgary College on a higher level in the popular imagination than the Strathcona institution, where the papers for degrees will probably consist of "Why is a hen?" "Who killed Cock Robin?" and kindred posers.

Strathcona degrees will soon become a joke. It is too near Ponoka (the Provincial Mental Hospital).

[*Bob Edwards' sample U. of A. exam*]

ENGLISH COMPOSITION

1. Write a 300 word eulogy on Principal Tory, and explain why he is.
2. Is what?
3. Parse sentence: "Good grammar teached here".
4. Is the word punk a predicate, superlative, or past participle?

HISTORY

1. Give brief history of Principal Tory.
2. When did Principal Tory draw up the Magna Carta?
3. Give date of Johnson-Jeffries fight.
4. How long did the Seven Years' War last?
5. Write what you know about Adam and Eve and their antecedents.
6. Give dates of Battle between Edmonton and South Edmonton for possession of Land Titles Office.

GEOGRAPHY

1. Where was Principal Tory born?
2. Name the principal rivers in Principal Tory's bailiwick.
3. Is Calgary on the map?
4. Name the capital of Alberta.

And of course the above are only a few samples, but they will give you a line on the outfit up north. Calgary College will now go ahead and erect a splendid institution on the heights overlooking the city and the valley of the Bow. The right men are behind it and will be more zealous than ever in furthering the interests of Caglary's seat of learning. They are now on their mettle.

After all, it's only the matter of a couple of years when there will be change of government, and then Calgary will come into her own as far as the University is concerned. So cheer up!
—*From* THE EYE OPENER, *1912.*

Built in 1905, the Cathedral Church of the
Redeemer is the centre for the Anglican diocese in
Calgary.

DAVID STERNTHAL

The clock tower of Calgary's first city hall.

DAVID STERNTHAL

The future meets the past. Calgary's new city hall stands out behind the old sandstone city hall.

DAVID STERNTHAL.

Dear Miss Dix:

I have a brother who earns a much bigger salary than I do. My mother is satisfied to have my brother pay her a fair board and have the rest of his money to spend as he pleases, but she makes me turn over my entire pay envelope to her and she gives me only back for my expenses what she thinks I should have. In a word, she considers that what my brother earns is his own, but what I earn belongs to her. When my brother comes home she thinks he should rest and she never asks him to do a thing about the house, but she demands that I help her get the dinner and wash the dishes afterward and help out with the sewing. Mother washes and mends my brother's clothes and keeps them looking tidy. I have to do my own. All of the girls that I work with have the same home conditions. Why do mothers treat their daughters so differently from their sons?

—Maud

Answer: Nobody knows, Maud. It is just the way mothers are built. A woman will offer her daughter up as a living sacrifice to the family...but she...calls upon the world to observe what a treasure heaven has blessed her with if her son does the smallest thing for her. Perhaps the reason that mothers are so much harder on their daughters is because the wage-earning girl is still so new that her mother has

Built in the 1880s, Stewart House was the home to one of Calgary's earliest entrepreneurs.

DAVID STERNTHAL

not yet had time to adjust herself to her. Perhaps, too deep for any one generation to eradicate it, there still lies the belief that a mother should control her daughter's expenditures. Mothers have not yet been able to see that when a girl becomes independent, her whole status in the household is changed and she should stand at least on an equal footing with her brothers.

Nor should a girl be expected to do housework after she has toiled all day. That is more than flesh and blood can stand. So many girls break down or fail to make good in

business because they are worn out doing double duty...The great majority of mothers still think that daughters should work both outside of the home and inside of it, while all that a boy should be expected to do is to enjoy himself after working hours.

And there you are, Maud. Brother will always be the fair-haired child with mother. She can't help it. It is biological.

—Dorothy Dix
THE CALGARY ALBERTAN
14 October 1929

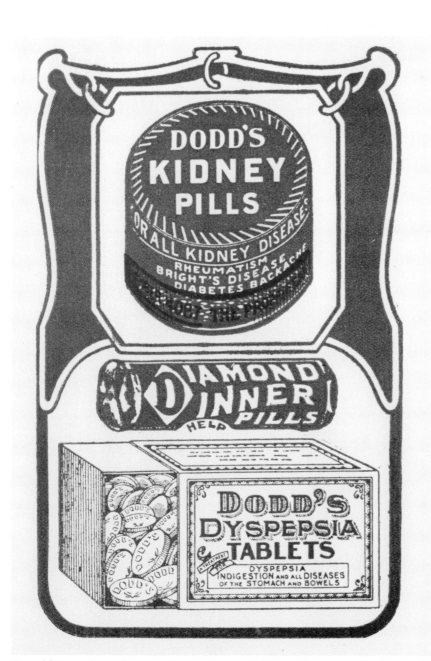

Pamphlets such as the one shown above reinforced the woman's place as in the home.

DAVID STERNTHAL

The altar of the Knox United Church, as viewed from the balcony.

DAVID STERNTHAL

The organ at Knox United Church in Calgary.

Interior of Cross House.

"It is astounding, when you come to think of it, how well this glorious country of ours seems to be getting along without old Bill Pugsley."
—*Bob Edwards,* SUMMER ANNUAL, 1921

A founding partner in Alberta's first oil and gas exploration company, and a backer of the original Stampede in 1912, A.E. Cross built his Calgary home in 1891.

DAVID STERNTHAL

93

DAVID STERNTHAL

The Memorial Park Library was the second library built between Winnipeg and the Rockies.

High-Grade Farm Wagons

GOOD wagons are absolutely necessary on the farm.

Remember that paint may hide a multitude of deficiencies—a lot of poor materials, particularly poor wood stock—and that the well painted but cheap and poorly constructed wagon may not be a bargain at any price. Break-downs are expensive, repairs cause delay, and in the end the cheap wagon will prove a most expensive one. Iron of the best quality; wood stock of desired toughness, thoroughly seasoned, are required for the big loads, rough roads, ruts, slips and slides that try the farm wagon.

The iron and wood must be put together properly to give the greatest durability.

That's not all; this excellence of material and building must be combined with light running qualities to make the completely successful farm wagon.

All these requirements you will find in the International Harvester Company line of farm wagons.

The Weber for more than fifty years has been among the best and most favorably known of America's farm wagons. The most carefully selected and seasoned materials with superior construction in every part make it suit every condition of wagon service.

The Columbus is a strong, well constructed and durable wagon, such as will well meet the needs of the great army of farm wagon buyers and users.

The Bettendorf is a new and valuable improvement in wagon construction, the front and rear gears being made entirely of pressed steel; therefore, the axles, bolsters and other gear parts are free from swelling, shrinking, rot, etc. Ideal for hot or dry climates.

They are the only steel constructed farm wagon gears on the market. These wagons are built to last. Almost any wagon can be guaranteed for a year, but the point that should always be considered is **how many years is the wagon likely to do good service?** Think it over. It makes little difference which of these wagons you buy. You will make sure of wagon value and wagon satisfaction in any event. You simply can't buy any thing better at any price.

Call on the local agent or write for illustrated pamphlets which fully describe each.

**Weber
Columbus
Bettendorf**

International Harvester Company of America

(Incorporated)   Calgary, Alta.

DAVID STERNTHAL

Colonel James Walker was one of Calgary's most colourful early mandarins. A N.W.M.P. officer, he later was involved with the railway, defended Calgary in the Northwest Rebellion, established the city's first telephone exchange and acted as a treaty commissioner for the federal government.

The Bow Valley Ranche house.

Front door detail of the Dominion Bank Building, Calgary.

PRAIRIE FIRE

The prairie fire seems to have started up at Olds and
came within 15 miles of Calgary. It is estimated that
20,000 tons of hay have been destroyed,
which is likely to have its effect on prices this winter.

—CALGARY HERALD, *21 October 1901.*

Cornice detail of the Alberta Historical Resources Building.

Calgary, Nov. 25, 1885

My dear Mr. Hardisty,

I indulge in the hope that you will be on your feet soon, or, as Shakespeare hath it, that ''Richard's himself again''—It appears to me that the Edmonton air does not fit you as well as the salubrious atmosphere of Calgary, eh? I have no doubt by this time you are in the throes of winter's chilly blast in Edmonton and that in the even-tide you gather around the blazing hearth and rub your hands and noses to the tune of ''Greenland's icy Mountains''—While we revel in sunshine, orange groves, banana fields, India's coral strand and Africa's sunny fountains—surprising the difference between the two points, eh? I always kept telling you Edmontonly disposed folks of this state of affairs, but of course you would not give attention to my sage remarks . . . .

How is sister Wood and her worthy expanse? I miss greatly the sociabilities which you carried off in your retinue when you left—Belle and I threaten at times to fall into a state of rust-dumbness by reason of having so few to brush elbows and tongues against—Hon. Donald A. was up here a few weeks ago. He telegraphed me to meet him at the station, I did so and we had quite a chat with the worthy driver of the last C.P.R. spike . . . .

I hope to see you down here shortly. I am postponing my Winnipeg trip to go down with you. Clara better pay us a visit when you come down—we shall be very much pleased if she does—Belle, baby & I send our affectionate regards to Mrs. Hardisty, Clara and Percy—Hoping that you will be at an early day strong and hearty again, Believe me, yours sincerely,

James A. Lougheed

—Letter from J.A. Lougheed (later senator and knighted by King George V) to Richard Hardisty, then Chief Factor for the Hudson's Bay Co. at Edmonton.

The front entrance to the Sir James Lougheed residence.

PRIZE LIST
"COME AN' GET 'EM!"

Cowboys' Bucking Horse Riding Contest for World's Championship—1st Prize, $1,000 cash and a fine saddle; 2nd Prize, $500.00 cash; 3rd Prize, $250.00 cash. Entrance fee, $25.00.

Cowgirls' Bucking Horse Riding Contest for World's Championship—1st Prize, $1,000.00 cash and a fine saddle; 2nd Prize, $500.00 cash; 3rd Prize, $250.00 cash. Entrance free.

Cowboys' Steer Roping Contest for World's Championship—1st Prize, $1,000.00 cash and a fine saddle; 2nd Prize, $500.00 cash; 3rd Prize, $250.00 cash. Entrance fee, $25.00.

This is for the average time on 3 steers. Additional prize of $500.00 to man making the fastest individual tie on one steer.

All cattle used in roping and bulldogging events will be from Old Mexico.

$200.00 cash prize for best roping horse.

$100.00 cash prize for best bucking horse and will buy him for $300.00 cash.

Cowboys' Contest in Steer Bulldogging for World's Championship—1st Prize, $500.00 cash and a fine saddle; 2nd Prize, $250.00 cash; 3rd Prize, $125.00 cash. Entrance fee, $12.50.

Cowboys' Contest Bareback Bucking Horse Riding with Sircingle for World's Championship—1st Prize, $500.00 cash; 2nd Prize, $250.00 cash; 3rd Prize, $125.00 cash. Entrance fee, $12.50.

Stage Coach Race—$250.00 Prize to winner. This amount is given each day. Entrance free.

Indian Relay Race—1st Prize, $100.00 cash; 2nd Prize, $60.00 cash; 3rd prize, $40.00 cash. Entrance free.

Cowboy Relay Race—1st Prize, $750.00 cash; 2nd Prize, $500.00 cash; 3rd Prize, $300.00 cash. Entrance fee, $25.00.

Nothing but saddle horses entered in this event. Professional race horses barred.

Cowgirl Relay Race—1st Prize, $500.00 cash; 2nd prize, $250.00 cash; 3rd prize, $125.00 cash. Entrance free.

Nothing but saddle horses entered in this event. Professional race horses barred.

Cowboy Fancy Roping Contest for World's Championship—1st Prize $500.00 cash and a fine saddle; 2nd Prize, $250.00 cash; 3rd Prize, $150.00 cash. Entrance fee, $12.50.

Cowboy Trick and Fancy Riding Contest for World's Championship—1st Prize, $500.00 cash and a fine saddle; 2nd Prize, $250.00 cash; 3rd Prize, $150.00 cash. Entrance fee, $12.50.

Cowgirl Trick and Fancy Riding Contest for World's Championship—1st Prize, $300.00 cash; 2nd Prize, $250.00 cash; 3rd Prize, $125.00 cash, Entrance free.

DAVID STERNTHAL

The sandstone window casement and parapet of the Thomson Brothers Block.

Wild Horse Race each Day by Cowboys—1st Prize, $100.00 cash; 2nd Prize, $50.00 cash; 3rd Prize, $25.00 cash.

This amount is given each day. Entrance fee, $10.00.

Various other liberal prizes given for the minor events. In any event where there are three cash prizes given there must be at least five entries.

Did you ever see a prize list like this before at a Frontier Day Celebration? No!

—*The prize list for the first Calgary Stampede, 1912.*

The facade of the L.H. Doll Building.

DAVID STERNTHAL

BOYS WILL BE BOYS

The boys have found a new and cheaper method of gaining admission to the opera house than by paying their money or begging a pass from everyone who attends. The new method is to enter by the coal cellar, and then to work their way up. They think it pretty small that Lippington is set to watch this handy mode of ingress, and they wonder if he remembers when he was a ''kid'' himself. The same youths held a meeting recently and appointed a committee to protest strongly against any action being taken about the establishment of a curfew bell, and strong resolutions were passed against either police or parents interfering with the liberties of free and independent ''kids'' born and cultured in the great ''woolly west.''
—CALGARY HERALD, *13 September 1895.*

Midnapore Lacombe Home
17 July 1909

The Honble. Rutherford
Prime Minister

My dear sir,
   You know already that we are beginning an establishment of a Home for the destitute, orphans, and other miserables of our Province of Alberta.
   Mr. Patrick Burns of Calgary have given the grounds for the institution. The sisters-managers are already arrived to begin the work; some friends and the public in general are very sympathetic to the undertaking.
   Therefor I take the liberty to apply to your government for help for the beginning. Your colleagues have encouraged me to make that application.
   Therefor as Prime Minister I hope you will do this thing for this work of humanity to help us during this season for the beginning.
   Thanking you beforehand, I remain very sincerely,

Truly yours
Father A. Lacombe
o.m.i.

The Lacombe Home in Midnapore. One of Alberta's best-loved pioneers and spiritual leaders, Father Albert Lacombe established the home for orphans and other destitute people in 1910.

Nimmons House. William Nimmons moved to the Calgary area in the early 1880s, and rode the crest of the development wave to early success.

DAVID STERNTHAL

Blood Agency,
Macleod, Alta,
July. 26th. 1912.

Guy. Weadick, Esq,
Manager The Stampede,
105 Eighth Avenue West,
Calgary, Alta.

Dear Sir,

Many thanks for the printed matter advertising the Stampede received here. In reply to your favour of the 20th inst there is only one Indian here who has made up his mind to enter and he wants to enter for the two bucking contests. He would like to know if the Stampede management provides the horses as it is impossible for him to get real bad ones down here and also has his entrance money to be in there by the 1st August. His name is Tom Three Persons of this Reserve . . . .

Yours faithfully,
Indian Agent.

Tom Three Persons won the world championship bucking horse contest at the first Calgary Stampede in 1912.

Millican House. Built by William Millican, the home was bought by the Nickle family in 1930.

BIG SKY

Look up. On the sun-soaked southern plains of Alberta, the horizon has no limits. The big sky dominates the landscape — a window to infinity. Below was the domain of Blackfoot, Blood and Peigan Indians.

The southern great plains were inhabited since prehistoric times with marginal impact on the natural environment. Only recently did proud buffalo hunters living by their own codes, give way to the intrusion of European culture. But the influences of industrialization and western civilization proved relentless. Guns, disease, railroads and alien settlement had their effects. The buffalo disappeared. The once-powerful Blackfoot Confederacy capitulated to the inevitable with the signing of Treaty Number Seven in 1877.

With the signing came the end of open space and the freedom to roam for both

DAVID CUNNINGHAM

Massacre Butte, near Cowley in the Crowsnest Pass. Though never documented, popular legend alleges that a group of American settlers were ambushed by Blood Indians at this site.

Indians and white men. Yet even though the southern plains are now, for the most part, surveyed, fenced, farmed, irrigated and grazed according to the rigid customs of Imperial land development, the sky remains without limits. Strangers, unused to confronting such vastness, dismiss the plains as "boring" as they drive toward more exotic locales. Those who have learned to accept the character of the plains know differently. When they get bored, they look up.

" I was lying in the snow watching a large herd of buffalo approaching. They stopped about five hundred yards from me and to my amazement I observed one of them was white as the snow it was travelling over. No, I don't mean that either; it was more a creamy white or light yellow. It was apparently a bull and full grown. I opened fire on the bunch trying, of course, to get a shot at the white one, but he was right in the middle of the bunch. There must have been thirty or forty buffalo between me and him, so I came to the conclusion that I'd have to kill off these in order to get the one I was after. I opened fire again and killed ten more. Just about the time I thought I'd get a shot at the white one, something or other startled the bunch and I never saw them again.

That was the only living white buffalo I ever saw. Some years later I did see two skins of albino buffalo in the I.G. Baker Company's store at Macleod, but the factor said that out of the thousands of hides the company handled at the Macleod store-house he had never seen white hides of buffalo excepting these two I speak of. I have seen white muskrats, beaver, and deer, but these too are very rare."
—*Kootenai Brown, "I remember,"* THE FARM AND RANCH REVIEW, *1919-1920.*

Now I am going to speak about how we lived Indian life. In the past people became Chiefs through wars. The reason why our grandfather Crowfoot became so famous they were on the war path, the war party said that striped designed tipi that's almost in the center, who is going to go forward and strike it, whoever goes forward and strikes it will be the chief of all the world and they made their decisions. I will make a run for it and he made a run for it and it was a Sun Dance and people were walking in all directions. The people were of different tribes nobody noticed him and when he struck it then he was noticed by the people and he fled out of the camps and he was almost ducking into the bush when everybody started shooting at him. He was shot in the leg and he was dragged into the bush and he was safe then. And thats how he became our grandfather! Crowfoot. The people in the past our grandfathers became chiefs by their battles. The one that does the most damage and apprehends the enemy will be the one that becomes chief. And then the wars stopped, then they didn't become chief by battles. After that a man becomes chief by his kindness and generosity and by his wealth and the holy things he endured and he is a chief and it stopped and it's there no more. And now today we have for chief the one that goes to high school.
— *Jack Big Eye, talking about Crowfoot, Blackfoot Reserve, 1965.*

DAVID CUNNINGHAM

The view from the Medicine Wheel on the Suffield Military Base. The exact role that these wheels played in early rituals is still uncertain.

An abandoned farmhouse near Massacre Butte.

"When slaughtering, the meat was usually divided among six people. One would take the heart and shoulder; another the loin and part of the innards; another the flank and ribs; another a hind quarter, paunch and fat; another hind quarter and entrails; and another the remainder. They would work together and each time a different portion was taken by each person."
—*Interview with John Cotton, Blood Indian aged 83, at Moses Lake Reserve January 5, 1957. Interviewed by Hugh Dempsey*

Looking down from the bluff of Head-Smashed-In Buffalo Jump.

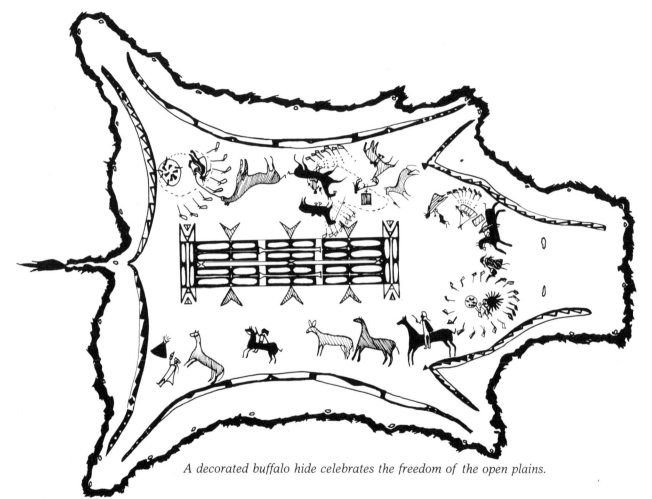

A decorated buffalo hide celebrates the freedom of the open plains.

I had a visit from Crowfoot, the chief of this portion of the Blackfeet. He brought a couple of his squaws along and a little child, a pretty little creature, whom he called *Pouse* after some kind of bird. I showed Crowfoot my paints and my sketches. I had one of himself; he recognised it immediately, as also did his squaws. Was that not a triumph of art? The old man had a bad headache so I gave him a Seidlitz powder; you should have seen his look of bewildered amazement as the powder began to fizz. He repeated over and over again, *Skoon-a-taps-saline*, which means ''very strong medicine''. Afterwards we regaled him with some Ginger Tea which elevated him so that he was almost tipsy. Then as it was lunch time I gave him and his squaws some bread and meat. They ate their fill and departed, shaking hands with every expression of delight.
—*R.B. Nevitt,* A WINTER AT FT. MACLEOD, *9 Feb. 1875.*

People started to exist that don't go through transferrals in No. 10, [1910] they followed the path of the white man's life, they got very wise, one of them is Big Sorrel Horse he didn't speak white man talk. The wise talk that the holy white man told him, his children were just going to school he was told to try hard to try and get wealthy so that after his children are educated they will have something to start with, that is how they were advised.

Big Sorrel Horse got very rich with the advice that was given to him that day. . . .

On the cold big holy day [Christmas] the holy white men will put up a feast, they will not treat a drunken person again the people tried hard not to get drunk that was a happy time. When the people all go to pray on Cold Big Holy Day bob sleighs some have double boxes they put some hay in the box.

People will camp by the dance hall for the Cold Big Holy Dance and nobody is drunk, the old people are just telling the people that drinking is bad. Whoever is going to drink, you know it is cold, those who have relatives, if they really pity their relatives they will report them and they will seized and they quit drinking and we have the dance, there is gaiety at the dance hall for the dances are quiet. . . .

And now today people have come to *atskonaisini* what we have reached today is very lonely, today is lonely with our holy white men

A primitive Indian doll, made from reeds.

[Priests] today is lonely with our seizers [Police] today is lonely with our curers [Doctors] today we have come to the point to always be crying about life, it is very grievous what shall we live for. Whatever is left of a person's property is all gone why were they all gone it's he is drinking continually, the reason why houses are vacant it's on account of drinking, the reason why people are dying it's on account of drinking.

Now today it has come back again people that are scared are dying of their hearts, the day that we have come to is very lonely, now myself that is how I am living now these stories that I am telling now are reminding me of the past, the happiness of the life of the past, the horses and cattle they are free on the plains. . . .

Today these are extinct people are drinking continually and I have a feeling that the last day is going to be here so now I finish my story at this point, I am very sorry for what I am telling about it is lonely, now I close my story I am First Rider that's all.
—*Interview with First Rider*

Hoodoo formations at Writing-On-Stone Provincial Park.

Petroglyphs (carved designs) in the soft rock at Writing-On-Stone Provincial Park. The practice of carving images into the stone dates back from 3,000 years ago to the present. The etching of men bearing shields is prehistoric, while the image of the wagon was carved after the arrival of the white men.

Feb. 25th [1841]—Nothing particular occurred. Heard that Indians say I came down from heaven in a bit of paper which was opened by one of the Co's gentlemen at the Forts & lo!! I came out.
—*From the Journal of Rev. Robert T. Rundle, Wesleyan missionary.*

DAVID CUNNINGHAM

Police Creek in Writing-On-Stone Provincial Park. A tributary of the Missouri River and just north of the U.S. border, the Milk River valley was an initial concern of the N.W.M.P. when they arrived in Alberta.

These patrols should visit isolated ranches and settlements and report on everything that has come under their observation, the police outfits they have met, freighters, travellers, movements of doubtful characters, condition of crops, prospects of hay, the ownership of any particularly fine horses they may see and to each report a rough map should be attached.
—*Circular memorandum, 12 April 1890. Instructions for N.W.M.P. patrols.*

Interior of Card House in Cardston. Mormon Charles Ora Card led a group of settlers to southern Alberta and established a community in 1887. The Mormons initiated the first irrigation projects in Alberta.

The Cardston Courthouse.

A man named Donaldson living there had made some filthy remark in connection with the name of a Miss Mary Macleod, sister of the ex-editor of the Cardston *Record*. The young lady compelled Mr. Donaldson at the muzzle of her revolver to make her an abject public apology which I understand he did in haste.

—*Ft. Macleod Monthly Report for the N.W.M.P., June 1900.*

1877 Dec. 10 Monday

Fine day—no wind—Rode down with Gladstone to see Crowfoot in his camp. He is suffering considerably with sciatia—found the drums going & medicine woman burning little holes in his leg along the course of the pain.

Dec. 11 Tuesday

A large fire burning on the prairie across the river north-east of us. A fire took place in John Smith's stables—the force turned out to put it out & soon succeeded. A very high wind sprung up suddenly about 11 a.m. & has continued all day.

Dec. 12 Wednesday

No news in particular today. One or two horse races gave an appearance of excitement to the little burgh—but it was evanescent. The Col. never sent for my drugs. I must get the order off by this mail. Crowfoot has been invited to stay in the Hospital while he is sick. What a lively hospital I will have in about a week!

—*From the Diary of R.B. Nevitt, N.W.M.P. Assistant Surgeon.*

The plains in winter.

Fire Hall Number One in Lethbridge is one of the oldest brick structures in southern Alberta.

Lethbridge Fire Hall cupola.

In the good old days when Alberta was dry, whiskey smugglers were sometimes caught ''with the goods.'' When practicable, the whiskey was usually brought into the post where it figured as ''Exhibit A'' against the prisoners. After having done duty as evidence, the kegs were usually knocked in at the head and the contents, under the direction of an officer, poured out on the ground. It frequently happened however, that after one of these ceremonies, the men seemed exceedingly jovial. In fact, their condition, had they been in a country where intoxicants were procurable, might have been ascribed to over indulgence.

The commanding officer in command of the post at Lethbridge at one time, noticed this peculiar fact, and decided that he would personally superintend the destruction of a certain large seizure. He would satisfy himself that orders were carried out in every detail. They were. Yet when ''stables'' were sounded that night, the sergeant-major, a seasoned veteran, was the only one to appear; and when he reported that all the men were laid out, the feelings of the commanding officer may be imagined.

He went to the spot where the liquor had been poured and investigated. The ground when he struck it with his stick, rang hollow. Further investigation revealed to the astounded officer the fact that from the interior of a building close by, a small tunnel had been burrowed beneath the place where the whiskey was spilled and receptacles placed so that they caught the precious fluid as it trickled through the thin covering above. That night there was mourning in the land and from that time on the interest of many a man in the chase was gone.
—LETHBRIDGE NEWS, *March 13, 1908.*

Window detail, Lethbridge Fire Hall.

MOVING PICTURES

The Edison Waragraph Company presented a large number of scenes and moving pictures to a fair audience last night. The views with the exception of a few were very plain, and could be spoken of as eclipsing anything of their nature ever shown here before.

After opening with a few pictures of scenes in Pretoria, Durban and other cities connected with the British-Boer war, the funeral of Queen Victoria was then brought on. In this could be seen many noted personages such as King Edward, the Emperor of Germany and others, as well as representatives from different foreign countries. This view although somewhat dim in some parts was very good, and from it one could conceive something of the magnificence and grandeur of the affair. Besides, a bird's eye view of the Paris Exposition, other interesting scenes at the Exposition were shown.

A large and varied selection of comic pictures, among which were "A Trip to the Moon," "Lovers Interrupted," "The Tricky Donkey," "The Haunted House" and "The One-Man Orchestra," created much laughter and amusement. Scenes in South Africa relating to the British-Boer war were looked upon with interest. M.J. Noel the famous Parisian specialty artist, impersonating a female, drew forth much applause. Another scene which was greatly appreciated by the audience was that of Mrs. Carrie Nation, and her brigade of Kansas saloon smashers at work.

The Company are holding a matinee in the hall this afternoon and will again show this evening with a change of programme, and judging from remarks heard will have a large audience.

—LETHBRIDGE NEWS, *6 June 1901.*

GUNFIGHT

LETHBRIDGE—Former City Detective Pat Egan was shot and perhaps wounded shortly after 7 o'clock Wednesday night in front of the Union Bank on the principal business street of the city by Richard Christian, a cowpuncher, who has been in the city for the past few days from the Iron Springs district. The shooting is said to be the result of an old feud between the two, Egan arrested Christian on several different occasions during the past two years. Christian is said to have made the remarks at each time that it would be only a short time until he would ''get'' him. The shooting was most sensational as the streets were crowded at the time with hundreds of pedestrians. The wounded man was shot in the back, about four inches below the right shoulder, the bullet coming out of his side near the top of the stomach, inflicting a severe intestinal wound.

After being shot Egan walked a short distance and asked for a gun. He staggered a short distance and just as he was falling was assisted by a number of bystanders, who rushed him across the street where medical attention was given. A few minutes later he was taken to the Galt hospital where it was necessary to perform an operation immediately.

Christian after firing the shot, started off in an opposite direction, running into the arms of Sergt. Kroning, of the police force, who pulled his gun and commanded him to throw up his hands. Christian handed over his gun and was escorted to the city police station where he was locked up in a separate cell, where he talked of the crime.

''Egan had ordered me out of town on several different occasions and at one time was instrumental in having me sent up for stealing a watch. When he passed me on the street he applied a vile name to me and I promptly pulled my gun and shot. I am not sorry that I shot him, and would do it again under the circumstances, as I will not take the name he called me under any circumstances from anyone, and if I was to swing for it tomorrow I would still be glad that I committed the deed.''

The prisoner is about 27 years of age, but states that he does not know how old he is, as he had never seen his father or mother to his recollection.
—CALGARY NEWS-TELEGRAM, *19 September 1912*

Around the Town

Messrs. Kelly & Young unloaded a carload of barbed wire yesterday.

Misses Hogg and Childs spent the weekend in town with friends.

Nurse Rodd of Vancouver, is a guest of her sister Mrs. F. Brazil at present.

Railways Rutherford and Roberts is the Liberal slogan in High River.

Duncan Marshall, of Olds, and L.M. Roberts spoke at a meeting held at Brant last night.

Ed. Welsh returned to High River on Tuesday after a prolonged visit to Oregon.

Miss Richards, who has been slightly indisposed for a week or so, resumed her work at Morrison & Co. this week.

Carpenters are at work on F. Tuck's barbershop, putting in a new frontispiece; when completed the Tuck barbershop will be a commodious one.

Parties desiring pullets had better put in their order to J.N. Partridge at once for he is making presents of them to his friends. Mr. R. Treacy was the lucky man to draw a pullet last week.

—HIGH RIVER TIMES, *11 March 1909.*

DAVID CUNNINGHAM

Column detail of the Bowman Arts Centre, Lethbridge.

The Hardie Residence in Lethbridge. W.D.L. Hardie was mayor of Lethbridge for 15 years.

An old dig at the Ross Site, south and east of Lethbridge. Archaeologists have excavated a prehistoric campsite here that dates back to 1,000 A.D.

The remains of St. Andrews Girls' Home.

Front door detail of the Medicine Hat Courthouse.

The Medicine Hat Courthouse.

"This being the only hospital between Winnipeg and Victoria patients came from long distances—Golden, Edmonton, Calgary, Macleod, Lethbridge, Grenfell, Prince Albert, Saskatoon and many intervening points of the C.P.R. A greater number of the patients were railway men and a greater part of the work was surgery. Dr. Calder was a clever surgeon.

At major operations the two doctors did the work, the matron gave the anaesthetic and the assistant was 'scrub up' nurse. The sterilizing of dressings, towels and instruments was done on the kitchen stove in saucepans and steamers as sterilizers were unknown at that time, at least as far as the North West Territories was concerned.

On one occasion an elderly man came in from Grenfell suffering from some abdominal trouble, the symptoms seeming to point to intestinal obstruction. It was decided to operate and they found a double intussusception about twelve inches apart which was removed.

There was no Murphy's button at their command so the ends of the intestine was sutured together and during the process the patient showed signs of collapse, everything had to be dropped and all attention given to reviving him. He soon rallied and after all washing and scrubbing preparations had been gone through again, the operation was completed. This had taken place in an empty room on the upper floor which he was to occupy. The assistant nurse was to stay and special him day and night for the first three days until he began to show signs of a steady improvement. Dr. Calder would come up to relieve the nurse for a half hour occasionally, but as to sleep she got what she could sitting in a rocker with a string attached to her wrist and the patient's which he promised to pull if he needed anything. He made a splendid recovery. . . ."

—*Miss E. Birtles, describing the Medicine Hat Hospital, c. 1890.*

123

On motion made and carried, it was re-solved that the seal of this company should be a circular design with the words *The Medalta Stoneware Limited* around the inner edge thereof, and the word ''incorporated'' and the figures ''1915'' across the centre of said design, and Secretary was ordered to impress the same upon the margin of the page of record book whereon these minutes are recorded.

—From the Minutes of the first meeting of the stock-holders of 22 December 1915 ''The Medalta Stoneware Ltd.''

Detail of kiln opening at Medalta Stoneware Ltd.

DAVID STERNTHAL

The Medalta Stoneware pottery kilns.

The Medicine Hat train station.

125

HOUSE RULES

1. Guests will be provided with breakfast and dinner, but rustle their own lunch.

2. Spiked boots and spurs must be removed at night before retiring.

3. Dogs not allowed in bunks, but may sleep underneath.

4. Towels changed weekly; insect repellent for sale at the bar.

5. Special rates to Gospel Grinders and the gambling profession.

6. The bar will be open day and night. Every known fluid, except water, for sale. No mixed drinks will be served, except in case of a death in the family. Only registered guests allowed the privileges of sleeping on the barroom floor.

7. No kicking regarding the food. Those who do not like the provender will be put out. When guests find themselves or their baggage thrown over the fence, they may consider they have received notice to leave.

8. Baths furnished free down at the river, but bathers must provide their own soap and towels.

9. Valuables will not be locked in the hotel safe, as the hotel possesses no such ornament.

10. Guests are expected to rise at 6 a.m., as the sheets are needed for tablecloths.

11. To attract the attention of waiters, shoot through the door panel. Two shots for ice water, three for a new deck of cards.

No Jawbone.

In God we trust; all others cash.

—House Rules of the Macleod Hotel, operated by Harry "Kamoose" Taylor in the 1880's. As related by J.B. Higinbotham.

May 19th

About nine o'clock this morning the wagons with our supplies began coming into the fort and the work of unloading and checking of the goods began. It took nearly the entire day to unload. There were eleven large wagons closely packed. I received a box of medicine which had been ordered last October. Do you not think that is very quick delivery? Nearly seven months. I begin to think I had better order my medicines for next winter immediately.

—From A.B. Nevitt, M.D., A Winter at Fort Macleod, *1875.*

Everybody waited for the train or stage coach to arrive to see if there were any unmarried girls coming to town. The old-timers at Macleod tell me that the arrival of the stage was the big moment for every bachelor in town.

Some of the more ardent bachelors would climb up the tops of houses and watch with field-glasses, to see if the stage was approaching. As it drew nearer, they could look inside and study the prospects. When at last it drew up in front of the hotel, there would be a regular stag-line of awkward, sun-tanned men, every one of them wondering whether his fate, his destiny, his future might not be stepping down onto the wooden sidewalk. . . .

In one case the bridegroom-to-be was a Mountie officer who went to great trouble to avoid being disappointed.

His bride was due in on the train. But he wasn't going to meet the train...no! He stationed himself on a hillside near the station armed with a powerful pair of binoculars. At last the train came in, and the bride-elect stepped down. Finding no one there to meet her, she walked up and down the platform.

Meanwhile, the Mountie had his binoculars trained upon her and was giving the lady a careful and thorough-going study. At last, he came to the decision that she wouldn't do. He dispatched his orderly with a note of regret and sufficient funds to send the woman back to her home.
—*"Laughter In The West"* OLD DAYS AND OLD TIMERS.

April 18, Wednesday, 1906
Did nothing very particular. Papa went to the bank etc. I took a photo of a lot of machinery. Terrific earthquake at San Francisco. Terrible damage done.
—*Unidentified diary of a new arrival to southern Alberta.*

The British Block Cairn on the Suffield Military Base. The cairn dates back to perhaps 3,000 B.C.

DAVID CUNNINGHAM

The "Big Rock," or the Okotoks Erratic.

DAVID CUNNINGHAM

GRASSLANDS

Farming remains the backbone of Alberta. To understand the character and heritage of those who developed this province, look to the small towns. Early settlers remembered their origins by naming their towns Viking, Hussar, New Norway and Innisfail. And they celebrated the bounty of the new land with such names as Cereal and Amber Valley. Rural communities throughout Alberta maintain religious customs, language, architecture and habits of nations often barely remembered by today's descendants.

Every year, the fields are sown and the crops harvested. No longer is the plow pulled by horse or man. No longer is the harvest dependent on itinerant steam threshers. Nowadays, phalanxes of combines swath hundreds of acres in single passes. But farmers still curse the elements, the cows are milked every morning, and dogs bark at the harvest moon. And the grain grows.

12th October—I started after breakfast to go to High River crossing to fetch back my luggage, and as things turned out I think this was the most eventful day of my life hitherto and had both a tragic and comical side to it, although I confess I did not appreciate the latter as much as anybody would have done who had been there to see some of it. Well, I had arranged to ride a four-year-old horse of Charlie's which had not been broken long, and to take with me an old horse called "Frenchie" which they said would be best to lead as a pack horse. I got off about 10 and all went well for about two miles when suddenly old Frenchie seemed to take it into his head that he had come far enough and stopped dead short and as I had got tight hold of the leading rein of course it pulled me head over heels backwards onto the ground, but luckily did not hurt me. The old brute having done this seemed perfectly satisfied and neither of them made any attempt to get away, although the black was quite loose. I got on again and made another start and the same game was repeated at intervals four times. I was afraid to let go of the rope for fear the old brute would bolt off and he really seemed to know this and how I ever got to the crossing I can't make out. My hands were all cut by the rope and I was sore all over and it really was a mercy that the black did not kick my brains out as I fell off on his heels every time. It took me just five hours to do the 12 miles, and how I was going to get back before dark I could not make out but I thought the old horse would be sure to go home all right, so I had a little to eat and got two fellows called Buck Smith and Tom Lynch to tie my pack onto Frenchy and off I started again.

I got about three miles all right when suddenly the pack rope broke and off fell the pack and away bolted old Frenchy as it was impossible to hold him. This seemed to frighten the black and he started to buck and shot me up into the air in a moment and landed me on my back and away he went also, leaving myself and the pack with no horse on the open prairie and late in the day. I could have cried with funk and vexation and sat there for some time not knowing what to do. At last I determined to try a trail which would lead me to some house, and after I had gone some distance I saw old Frenchy standing still grazing and thought I would try and catch him, and when I got up to him I found that the broken rope had got tangled around his hind legs and had hobbled him. This was very lucky so I cut the rope away and got on him and then didn't I vent my feelings on the old brute with my quirt. I then rode on for about three miles to the river until I came to a house where I found a very civil man who said he would come with me and fetch my pack and then try and find the black horse. We first

A lonely tree grows on the prairies.

rode off towards where I had left the pack but on the way he said he thought he saw the black in the distance so we rode off and got around him and he roped him. We then went and found the pack and he conveyed us all to Skrine's ranch about five miles away. It was 6:45 p.m. when I got to Skrine's thoroughly beaten and I really don't know what I would have done but for the man who was most kind and whose name I hear is "Holmes" and is nicknamed "Bar D." I got some supper as soon as I could and then went to bed with a splitting headache.
—*From the 1886 journal of J.L. Douglas, visiting Alberta from England.*

An abandoned shack nears collapse.

The weathered wood tells the story of the elements.

Chalmers Church Notes

Subjects for Sabbath, January the tenth, morning, "Joys and Sorrows of a Prison House," evening; "Abraham, as a Business Man."

If you are looking for work that will bring the most enduring turns you will find a place on our Sabbath School Staff.
—HIGH RIVER TIMES, *7 January 1909*

The Rev. John McLean of Cayley will preach next Sabbath, both morning and evening. Mr. McLean has resigned his charge and expects to go to Vancouver in March. Mrs. Wallace was at home to the choir on Thursday evening last. A most delightful evening was spent and all enjoyed themselves to the full.

The presbytery of High River meets at Granum, on Wednesday afternoon the 17th.

Mr. D.H. Campbell, of Kamloops, B.C., was a visitor at the manse, last week.
—HIGH RIVER TIMES, *11 Feb. 1909.*

131

Dr. Henry George's Residence near Innisfail. Arriving in Canada in 1889, Dr. George served as Assistant Surgeon to the N.W.M.P. before starting a practice at Innisfail in 1893.

The Hiebert Residence displays the circular verandah popular in early Alberta homes.

In speaking of the recent visit to Wetaskiwin of Lemen Bros.' circus, the Free Lance, published at that place, pays the following delicate tribute to the N.W.M. Police: ''It may not be out of place in these columns to say a word in praise of the tactful manner in which the N.W.M. Police perform their duties on occasions of this kind, when the fears of the public on the score of an invasion of dangerous toughs are but too well grounded. Moving about in an unobtrusive way, chatting with friends, laughing when there is something to laugh at, putting on no bogus airs, hunting no trouble, they are ready should trouble arise, to attend to it on the instant in a very thorough-going manner. The iron hand in a glove of velvet should make a good crest for the N.W.M.P.''
—MACLEOD GAZETTE, *Sept. 16, 1898.*

Old Main Building at Camrose Lutheran College.

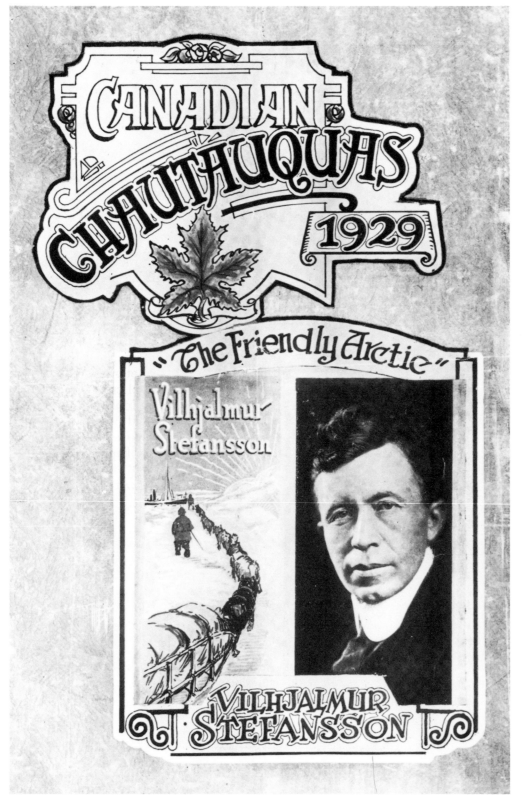

IAN SCOTT

The train statin on the C.P.R. main line at Suffield.

"It was amusing getting off at various stations to stretch one's legs. There's always a crowd of spitting, chewing loiterers waiting for the train to come in. . . . These little prairie townships are much the same—real estate office, hotel, livery barn, general store, a few shacks, and generally a church and school."
—*J. Burger Bickersteth,* THE LAND OF OPEN DOORS, *1911.*

Travelling Chataqua Shows toured Alberta in the 1920s and 1930s, bringing world-class culture to developing areas. The 1929 show featured Arctic explorer Vilhjalmur Stefansson, Canadian-born.

THE U.F.A. PATTERN DEPARTMENT

Send orders to *The U.F.A.* Pattern Department Lougheed Building, Calgary, allowing five days for receipt of pattern. Be sure to give name, address, size and number of pattern required. In some cases the customs office requires payment of seven cents duty on delivery.

7026. Ladies' Dress.

Designed in Sizes: 34, 36, 38, 40 and 42 inches bust measure. It requires 4 5/8 yards of 39 inch material for a 38 inch size. Vestee of contrasting material requires 1/2 yard 18 inches wide cut lengthwise. Price 15¢.

7047. Girls' Dress.

Cut in 5 Sizes: 1, 2, 3, 4, and 5 years. A 2 year size with bishop sleeves requires 1 3/4 yard 35 inches wide. With puff sleeves 1 3/8 yard will be required. To trim as illustrated requires 9 yards of banding (or insertion) and 2 7/8 yards of edging. Price 15¢.

—From THE UFA *newspaper, 1931. The United Farmers of Alberta gave rural Alberta a political voice, and also served as social and cultural communication network.*

Wide-awake women realized that back of their special problems—the efficient management of the home, and the training and care of children—lay the economic problem. Labor-saving devices, conservation of health, better rural schools and higher education were directly connected with better markets, co-operative buying and selling, and better agricultural credit. In other words, the farmer's problem was his wife's problem also. What could be more logical than for her to assist the farmers' movement? And that is exactly what happened.
—WORKING HINTS FOR LOCAL UNIONS OF THE UNITED FARM WOMEN OF ALBERTA *U.F.W.A. pamphlet.*

News of U.F.A. Locals

Rolling Green U.F.A. Local has passed a resolution protesting ''against the savage attack made upon Carl Axelson and freedom of speech.''

H.M. Brown, secretary of Hand Hills Lake U.F.A. Local writes that two get-together socials have been held since the New Year, both successful in every way.

McCafferty U.F.A. Local held its annual cribbage tournament recently; the beautiful engraved cup went to the vice-president, John Cram, an old timer and a faithful U.F.A member.

''We have just unloaded a big car of flour for $1.60 per cwt.'' writes W.A. Isaac, secretary of Consort U.F.A Local. ''People are well pleased with it, and the co-op. are ordering three more cars.''

Urging that the present financial situation ''is proof that privately owned banks have failed to serve the masses of the people,'' a resolution from Chinook U.F.A. Local approves ''the plan of nationalization of credit as set forth by Mr. George Bevington.''

In memory of the late J.W. Simmons, of Carstairs, the annual meeting of Beaver Dam municipality passed a standing vote of appreciation of this ''old resident and esteemed citizen who gave of his best for the economic advancement of his fellow men'' and extended sincere sympathy to the bereaved family.

Hansen's Corner U.F.A. Local, formed last June, holds monthly meetings, reports Walter C. Allen, secretary, ''all members showing a keen interest and a truly co-operative spirit.'' In addition to several dances and a whist drive, the entertainment committee arranged a fine concert on January 30th, given to a packed house.

Rosehaven Normal School in Camrose.

DAVID STERNTHAL

136

Ribstones. These strangely carved rocks were probably important in ancient buffalo-hunt rituals.

DAVID CUNNINGHAM

SYNOPSIS OF CANADIAN NORTH-WEST LAND REGULATIONS.

ANY person who is the sole head of a family, or any male over 18 years old, may home-stead a quarter section of available Dominion land in Manitoba, Saskatchewan or Alberta. The applicant must appear in person at the Dominion Land Agency or Sub-agency for the district. Entry by proxy may be made at any agency, on certain conditions by father, mother, son, daughter, brother or sister of intending homesteader.

Duties.—Six months' residence upon and cultivation of the land in each of three years. A homesteader may live within nine miles of his homestead on a farm of at least 80 acres solely owned and occupied by him or by his father, mother, son, daughter, brother or sister.

In certain districts a homesteader in good standing may pre-empt a quarter-section along-side his homestead. Price $3.00 per acre.

Duties.—Must reside upon the homestead or pre-emption six months in each of six years from date of homestead entry (including the time required to earn homestead patent) and cultivate fifty acres extra.

A homesteader who has exhausted his home-stead right and cannot obtain a pre-emption may enter for a purchased homestead in certain districts. Price $3.00 per acre. Duties.—Must reside six months in each of three years, culti-vate fifty acres and erect a house worth $300.00.

W. W. CORY,

Deputy of the Minister of the Interior.

N.B.—Unauthorized publication of this ad-vertisement will not be paid for.

Barn near Killam.

DAVID CUNNINGHAM

"On January 9th, at Meadowbrook Community Hall, was held the annual rally of Gleichen U.F.A. and U.F.W.A. Locals, when 170 persons partook of the 8 p.m. dinner. A splendid program was put on, including a play by local school-children, and the crowd swelled to around 250 for the dance. At this affair everything is free, but it is understood that the ladies will bring enough food for those in their own parties. We haven't seen fit to limit the welcome to members only as the pleasure of the occasion is an inducement to outsiders to join.'—H.H. Ellis, Secretary U.F.A. Local.

Plans to Foster Co-operative Movement in Alberta
Alberta Co-operative Council Considers Proposals—Officers of Council Elected

Steps to strengthen and enlarge the scope of the co-operative movement in Alberta were considered at a meeting of the Alberta Co-operative council on February

24th and 25th, and as a result of the meeting a number of suggestions were made to the U.F.A. Executive—the U.F.A. Central Board, acting on instructions of the Annual Convention, having been the body by whom the initial steps in the matter were taken some weeks ago.

H.E.G.H. Scholefield, who has been chairman of the Council since its formation, retired from this position, stating that in view of the circumstance that all members are required under the constitution to be representatives of Province-wide bodies engaged in co-operative activity, his relinquishing of the Vice-Presidency of the U.F.A made a new appointment desirable. Very high appreciation of the services rendered by Mr. Scholefield was expressed by the Council. Norman F. Priestley, Vice-president of the U.F.A., was unanimously elected chairman of the Council, as were the following Executive members: Norman F. Clarke, Didsbury and H.B. MacLeod, High River.

—From The *UFA (newspaper), 2 March 1931.*

Ask Government to Take Action at Once to Abolish Beer Parlors
Convention, by Majority, Passes Resolution

After debating the question from many angles, the Convention passed, by a rather large majority, the following resolution which originated in Sturgeon Provincial C.A.

Whereas, the beer halls continue to be a menace to the social and economical life of the Province, and

Whereas, the U.F.A. and U.F.W.A. Convention have passed strong resolutions condemning the beer halls and asking the Government for a plebiscite, and

Whereas, the Alberta Prohibition Association have initiated and circulated a petition under direct legislation this year in Alberta asking the Government to abolish beer halls;

Therefore be it resolved, that we endorse their request for legislation and also heartily endorse the request made through the petitions of the Alberta Prohibition Association that the government take action at once to abolish the beer parlors either by legislation or a plebiscite.

The mover of the resolution stated that it only asked the Convention to reaffirm the stand taken the year before and maintained that the beer parlors were "becoming worse and worse." He was referring to the distribution of beer during the last election campaign when called to order by the chairman.

—From The UFA, *2 Feb. 1931.*

Weather—last night was the coldest for years. The temperature went down to 55 below during the night. It was very misty during the forenoon but cleared up a bit in the afternoon. Temperature low throughout west.
—*Monday 28 January 1929*, MIDLAND
COAL JOURNAL, *Drumheller*

Snow fence.

IAN SCOTT

HISTORIC SITES
OF ALBERTA

Column detail of the Royal Bank Building, Calgary.

NORTHERN ALBERTA
HISTORIC
RESOURSES

★ Site with interpretation

☆ Site without formal interpretation

⊗ Site not open to public

```
0          100          200
|----------|----------|
KILOMETRES
```

High Level

Fort Vermilion
⊗ Old Bay House
⊗ Sheridan Lawrence Ranch

Bitumount
Oil Extraction Plant ⊗

Peace River

Hay River

Manning
☆ Plavin Homestead

Fort McMurray

Athabasca

Peace R.
Fairview
⊗ St. Augustine Mission
Peace River
Dunvegan
⊗ Factor House
Falher
St. Jean Baptiste RC Ch.
Grouard ☆ St. Bernard Mission
Grande Prairie
⊗ Rev. Forbes Homestead
Valleyview
Smoky River
Grande Cache
Whitecourt
St. Peter's Anglican Church (Lac La Nonne)
St. Albert
Lac La Biche
Cold Lake
Athabasca
Westlock
Hinton
Edson
Vermilion   Lloydminster
☆ Grizzly Bear

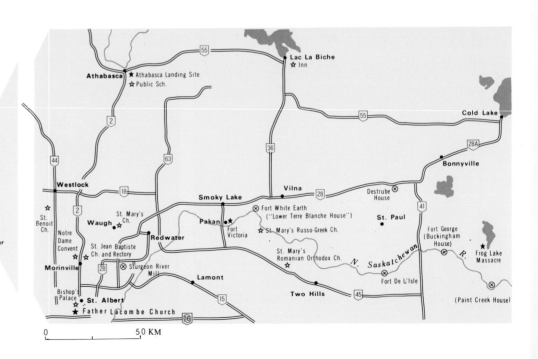

Athabasca   ★ Athabasca Landing Site
☆ Public Sch.

Lac La Biche
☆ Inn

Cold Lake

Westlock

Smoky Lake   Vilna
Destrube House ⊗

Bonnyville

⊗ Fort White Earth ("Lower Terre Blanche House")
Pakan ★
☆ St. Benoit Ch.
Waugh ☆   St. Mary's Ch.
Fort Victoria
☆ St. Mary's Russo-Greek Ch.
St. Paul

Notre Dame Convent
Redwater
St. Jean Baptiste Ch. and Rectory
⊗ Sturgeon River Mill
Morinville
St. Mary's Romanian Orthodox Ch. ☆

Fort George (Buckingham House)
★ Frog Lake Massacre

N. Saskatchewan R.
⊗ Fort De L'Isle

Bishop's Palace
● St. Albert
★ Father Lacombe Church
Lamont
Two Hills
(Paint Creek House) ⊗

```
0          50 KM
|----------|
```

Fort Vermilion, or Paint Creek House
North bank of North Saskatchewan River, opposite mouth of Vermilion River

Two posts, both known as Fort Vermilion, were established about 1802 within a single palisade, one operated by the North West Co., the other by the Hudson's Bay Co. Both traded with the Blackfoot and Cree Indians until 1816. Their closure left Fort Augustus and Fort Edmonton as the principal posts on the upper Saskatchewan.

Frog Lake Massacre
2 km south of Frog Lake

During the Northwest Rebellion, on April 2, 1885 a group of Cree warriors from Big Bear's camp, goaded by the attitudes of Indian Agent Thomas Quinn and Farm Instructor John Delaney, killed nine of the white settlers at this small settlement. Among the dead were Delaney and Quinn, and fathers Fafard and Marchand. Seven of the nine are buried in a small cementery near the lake.

Fort de l'Isle
North of Myrnam, on Fort Island in the North Saskatchewan

Alexander Mackenzie, nephew of the famous explorer who reached both the Arctic and the Pacific oceans from the Athabasca region, established the first post on Fort Island in the winter of 1799-1800 for the renegade XY Co. Competitors from the Hudson's Bay and North West companies immediately set up competitive posts on the island, but by 1902 all the posts had closed in favour of Fort Vermilion.

St. Mary's Romanian Orthodox Church
At Boian, east of Willingdon

Romanian pioneers began to settle at Boian, named after a village in Bukovina, in 1898. St. Mary's — built in 1903, completed and blessed in 1905 — is one of the oldest Romanian Orthodox churches still in use in Canada. The church was designed according to Romanian Byzantine tradition and built out of logs, which were given a wood siding in 1918 and a stucco finish in 1948.

Fort White Earth-Lower Terre Blanche House
14 km southeast of Smoky Lake

In the winter of 1809-10, the North West Co. abandoned the first Fort Augustus and Fort Vermilion for economic reasons and built a post here. In an unusual example of co-operation, the Hudson's Bay Co. followed the North West Co.'s move and built its fort in the same stockade. Both forts were abandoned in 1813.

he was forced for financial reasons to close the inn, which in 1936 was converted into Ste. Catherine's Hospital.

Bitumount Oil Sands Plant
70 km north of Fort McMurray, 30 km north of Highway 963

R.C. Fitzsimmons set up his first rudimentary permanent hot-water extraction plant in 1930 to remove oil from the oil sands. Despite later improvements to the plant, Fitzsimmons was forced to sell out to Montreal financier Lloyd Champion in 1943. Champion persuaded the Alberta government to develop a larger demonstration plant, which eventually operated in 1948 and 1949.

Grizzly Bear Telegraph Station
30 km southeast of Vermilion

The Dominion Telegraph Line was built in the early 1870s, following the northern route first proposed for the C.P.R. In 1876-77 the Grizzly Bear Telegraph Station opened, probably not to transmit or receive messages, but to accommodate those who maintained the lines. It closed in 1887, after both the railroad and the telegraph line were realigned to the south.

Fort George/Buckingham House
10 km east-southeast of Elk Point

Four months after James Hughes of the North West Co. founded Fort George in 1792, William Tomison of the Hudson's Bay Co. built Buckingham House next to it. Although commercial rivals, the forts shared a common well. After the traders abandoned the posts to move to Fort de l'Isle, the two forts closed in 1800.

Destrube House
At Rife, west of Bonnyville

The four Destrube brothers (Maurice, Georges, Guy and Paul), were reputedly the first white settlers in the Bonnyville area, opening a trading post in 1907. Maurice built this two-storey log farmhouse in 1913-14 to his brother Georges' design with a finely-finished interior ceiling and split-stone fireplace.

St. Mary's Russo-Greek Orthodox Church
At Shandro, 14 km north of Willingdon

The first Ukrainian settlers began arriving in Alberta in 1892. The Shandro clan was primarily reponsible for building St. Mary's between 1902 and 1904. A bell tower was added about 1915. The church is an excellent example of vernacular Bukovynian Byzantine architecture, fashioned of logs covered with wood siding. The first burial took place in the graveyard in 1901.

McArthur Hotel, or Lac La Biche Inn
Lac La Biche

J.D. McArthur, who undertook to construct a number of northern Alberta railways under provincial charter, was convinced before World War I that the Lac La Biche region had good tourist potential. He commissioned architect Roland W. Lines to design a hotel, and imported French workers to build it. By 1918

Fort Victoria
12 km south-southeast of Smoky Lake

William Christie, Fort Edmonton's chief factor, established Fort Victoria in 1864 to respond to pressure from the free traders. Only the clerk's house, a structure featuring post-on-sill design, remains.

Bishop's Palace/Grandin House
5 Rue St. Vital
St. Albert

Intended as a convent and hospital for the Grey Nuns from Montreal, Bishop's Palace became the residence of Bishops Grandin and Vital. Construction dragged on from 1882 to 1887, disrupted in part by the Northwest Rebellion. When the episcopal see was moved to Edmonton in 1912, the building became a home for retired Oblates and the rectory for St. Albert's parish priests.

St. Jean-Baptiste Roman Catholic Church and Rectory
10034 and 10020 100 Ave., Morinville

The Morinville and St. Jean-Baptiste parish was established in 1891 by Father Jean-Baptiste Morin. The present church, constructed in 1907 and given its brick veneer in 1929, replaced an earlier log structure dating from 1893. The rectory was built in two phases, with the second presbytery added to the 1895 presbytery in 1912.

Le Moulin de St. Christophe/ Sturgeon River Mill
Sturgeon River, near Bon Accord

In 1870, the new mission of St. Albert was raised to the dignity of an episcopal see. In 1878, the prospering mission's inhabitants successfully petitioned for a new grist mill on the Sturgeon River. A circular saw, planer and shingle machine were soon added. Only some collar pits, small segments of two dams, a man-made lagoon and a flume remain to mark the historic site.

St. Benoit Church
Main Street, Pickardville

Designed by Father Henri Garnier and built in 1929 to replace the original built in 1911, this church with its 38-m steeple is Pickardville's most prominent man-made landmark. Before it burned down, this church stood for the long history of the Roman Catholic mission and French Canadian settlement in the area.

Athabasca Landing Site
Athabasca

Athabasca Landing grew around a large warehouse built by the Hudson's Bay Co. in 1877, after completing a new road from Fort Edmonton to the elbow of the Athabasca River, the water terminus for the vast northland beyond. The river's second steamboat, the *Athabasca*, began to ply the river between Mirror Landing and Grand Rapids in 1888.

St. Bernard Roman Catholic Mission
Grouard

This mission was built in 1902 by chief carpenter Brother Dumas (under the direction of Bishop Emile Grouard) as the cathedral for his Athabasca-Mackenzie vicariate. An accomplished artist, Bishop Grouard painted the altar mural of the Crucifixion. One of four bishops buried in the mission cemetery, Grouard set up a press to translate prayer books into Cree and Beaver.

Father Lacombe Church
7 Rue St. Vital
St. Albert

Alberta's oldest surviving building, the church was built about 1861 by the Oblate missionary Father Albert Lacombe (1827-1916). The single-storey log building was used as a church until 1870, and thereafter as a sacristy, storehouse, granary, and finally, a museum since 1929.

Notre Dame Public School/ Convent
10010 101 St., Morinville

Built in 1909 as the convent of the teaching order of Les Filles de Jesus, the school/convent eventually became part of the Place St. Jean, a downtown cultural and recreational facility in Morinville, together with the St. Jean-Baptiste Church and Rectory. Two annexes were built in 1920 and 1930. Until 1972, this was the Order's provincial house.

St. Mary's Church
22 km north of Bon Accord, 18 km east of Highway 2 Waugh

Since it was built between 1904 and 1909, during the area's earliest settlement period. St. Mary's has been connected with the Ukrainian Catholic community. Until a new St. Mary's was built in 1940, members travelled considerable distances to attend services in their pioneer log church graced with an onion cupola dome, symbol of the Trinity.

Athabasca Public School
4710 48 St., Athabasca

Roland Lines, architect of the McArthur Inn at Lac La Biche, also designed Athabasca Public School in 1913. The impressively-sized school of Calgary red brick and Bedford limestone reflects the optimism of a small northern town's citizens, as they planned for their future education needs.

St. Peter's Anglican Church
Lac La Nonne

St. Peter's was established by local Anglican settlers with the assistance of a clergyman supported by the English Archbishops' Western Canada Fund. Rev. W.G. Boyd was placed in the huge Edmonton mission west of the city in 1910, and this church was built by volunteer labour in 1911 on land donated by settler Robert Hombling, showing an effective combination of English mission and local effort.

Forbes Residence
10424 96 St., Grande Prairie

Reportedly the only log building still on its original site in Grande Prairie, this building was constructed of spruce logs by Rev. and Mrs. Alexander Forbes in 1911 to serve as the first hospital in the town. In 1912 they added a two-storey manse to the structure. Subsequent exterior renovations have retained the basic architecture.

St. Jean-Baptiste Roman Catholic Mission
4 km south of Falher

Brother Dumas, an Oblate from St. Bernard Mission at Grouard, built this church in 1914 with local and Mission assistance to replace a smaller sod-roof log church. With a priest's residence above the church, it served the settlers of the Falher, Girouxville and Donnelly areas from 1914 to 1919.

Fort Dunvegan Factor's House
Foot of Dunvegan Bridge, near Fairview

Archibald Norman McLeod, senior wintering partner in the North West Co., established Fort Dunvegan in 1805. Long after the North West Co. amalgamated with the Hudson's Bay Co., Fort Dunvegan's transportation and agricultural importantance was recognized by the replacement of the old buildings with new, of which the 1877-78 factor's house remains.

St. Augustine Roman Catholic Mission
Peace River, in Shaftesbury Settlement

The original St. Augustine's Mission was built on the flats at Strong Creek by the Oblate Order in 1888. Relocated in 1892, the extant church was completed in 1896. Until 1950, the Sisters of Providence ran the major educational institute and the hospital facilities which were (until the 1930s) the only ones in the immediate vicinity.

Plavin Homestead
8.5 km south of Manning

The buildings on the homestead of Charles Plavin, a Latvian stonemason who settled in the North Star area south of Manning in 1918, display his craftsmanship and ingenuity. The house features hand-made doors, bookcases and furniture, a stone fireplace-furnace and a sauna. Plavin's commitment to music resulted in support for musical education.

Old Bay House
Fort Vermilion

The Old Bay House is the last remaining structure from this Hudson's Bay Co. post on the Peace River from 1830 to the 1970s. Built as part of the replacement programme at Fort Vermilion around 1900, it served as factor's residence until the 1930s.

Sheridan Lawrence Ranch
Near Fort Vermilion, on the Peace River

The Lawrence family came from Ontario in 1879 and later established one of the earliest, most successful independent ranching and trading operations in the north Peace Country. At its peak, the ranch had 1,000 acres, 35 buildings and two steamboat landings. The Lawrences established the farm and taught at the first Anglican mission at Fort Vermilion, and helped to build other missions.

Grant McConachie House
12909 121 St.
Edmonton

This is the childhood home of Grant McConachie, who launched his aviation career in 1931 as a bush pilot flying tough northern routes. He later joined Canadian Pacific Airlines, then served as president of Pacific Western Airlines from 1947 until his death in 1965.

Magrath Mansion
6240 Ada Blvd.
Edmonton

One of the grandest mansions built in the pre-World War I boom in Edmonton, this was the home of realtor W.J. Magrath from 1912 to 1920. An architectural landmark in Magrath's Highlands Subdivision, it has oak panelling, a winding staircase, linen wall-coverings, parquet floors, sculptured ceilings and beautiful built-in furniture in the dining room and library.

Ravina Apartments/McIntosh Residence
10325 Villa Ave.
Edmonton

The year realtor John McIntosh built his residence, 1912, was also the year he brought the Hudson's Bay Reserve onto the market, helping precipitate Edmonton's great land boom. H.A. Magoon designed the brick house with a hip roof, since replaced with a gable roof and dormer windows. The building was converted into apartments in 1920.

LeMarchand Mansion
11523 100 Ave.
Edmonton

René LeMarchand came to Edmonton in 1905, profited from the land boom, and then built this mansion with financial backing from a Paris café waiter's union. Considered in its day to be *the* apartment building in town, it was designed in "French Romantic" by A.M. Calderon and completed in 1911 by building contractor and former mayor Charles May.

St. Joachim's Roman Catholic Church
9920 110 St.
Edmonton

Bishop Tache originally gave Fort Edmonton's Roman Catholic mission the name of St. Joachim in 1854. The present church, the third St. Joachim's, was designed and built by Francis X. Deggendorfer in 1898-99. The sacristy was added in 1912. Inside, the elaborately-decorated wood panelling is illuminated by exceptionally well-crafted leaded stained-glass windows.

Prince of Wales Armory
10440 108 Ave.
Edmonton

The Prince of Wales Armory was completed for infantry regiments in 1915. It features the Medieval Revival design of David Ewart, chief architect with the Dominion government, and his local assistant, E.C. Hopkins. The 101st Regiment, the Edmonton Regiment, the Loyal Edmonton

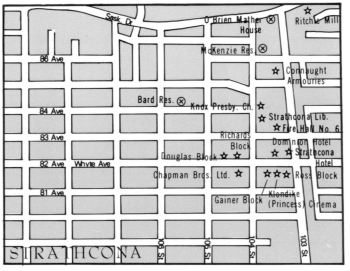

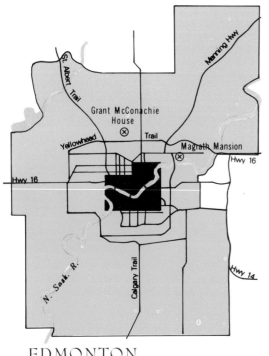

EDMONTON

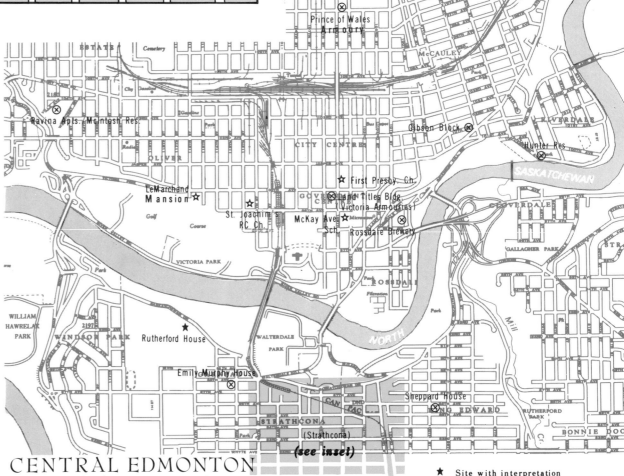

CENTRAL EDMONTON
HISTORIC
RESOURSES

★ Site with interpretation
☆ Site with no formal interpretation
Site not open to public

Regiment and the Edmonton Fusiliers have all been based here.

First Presbyterian Church
10025 104 St.
Edmonton

The Edmonton (Strathcona) firm of Wilson and Herald designed this Presbyterian Church built in 1911, the third to be constructed on the site. Between the years 1883 and 1930, Rev. D.G. McQueen, a leading force in the Presbyterian Church in Canada, conducted services at all three.

Land Titles Office
10523 100 Ave.
Edmonton

Dating from 1893, this building anticipated the land boom that would soon hit Edmonton. It served as a Crown land, timber and registry office for several years, but it was also referred to as Victoria Armories as a result of its occupation during World War I by the 19th Alberta Dragoons and during World

War II by the Edmonton Fusiliers.

MacKay Avenue School
10425 99 Ave.
Edmonton

Despite the spelling error in the name carved above the front entrance of this 1904 school, both it and its 1881 predecessor situtated nearby were named after W.H. MacKay, a prominent pioneer doctor. Designed by Edmonton architect H.D. Johnson, the red brick and sandstone school was selected as the site for the first two sessions of the Alberta Legislature (1906-1907).

Rossdale Brewery
9843 100 St.
Edmonton

The oldest unaltered brewery in the province was originally built in 1898 as the home of the Edmonton Brewing and Malting Co. The business failed, but was revived in 1904 by W.H. Sheppard, whose use of a "Budweiser" label proved controversial. The former brewery eventually became

an automobile repair shop.

Gibson Block, or Flatiron Building
9608 Jasper Ave.
Edmonton

William Gibson, a city realtor, had this block designed for him by N.W. Cowley in 1913. Intended as an office building, it was converted early to apartments and rooms for rent. A Turkish bath operated in the basement after 1914. Originally a highly fashionable building, with mosaic floors and oak panelling, it had the distinctive triangular shape once found in many North American cities.

Hunter Residence
9351 Cameron Ave.
Edmonton

Built around 1907 by contractor Alexander McKay, this large-scale wooden home commands a fine view over the North Saskatchewan River. The property was once owned by Frank Oliver, editor of the *Edmonton Bulletin* and Minister of the Interior in the federal cabinet of 1905-1911.

Rutherford House
11153 Saskatchewan Dr.
Edmonton

Dr. A.C. Rutherford, the province's first premier from 1905 until his resignation in 1910, had this house built in 1911. Responsible for the creation of the University of Alberta, he served 20 years on its senate and was its chancellor from 1927 until he died in 1941.

Emily Murphy House
11011 88 Ave.
Edmonton

An author and social conscience well ahead of her time, Emily Gowan Murphy lived in this 1912 house from 1919 until her death in 1933. A powerful advocate of equality for women, Murphy is best remembered for her part in the so-called "Person's Case" which led to the judgement in 1929 that women were actually "persons" who could be called to the Canadian Senate like men.

Sheppard House
9945 86 Ave.
Edmonton

After his arrival in 1894, W.H. Sheppard owned and operated several hotels in the Strathcona area. In 1904 he opened the Edmonton Brewery in Rossdale Flats, and two years later was mayor of Strathcona. He built his two-and-a-half storey brick house in 1912, at a time of expansion for Strathcona, about to amalgamate with Edmonton.

O'Brien/Mather House
10311 Saskatchewan Dr.
Edmonton

Years after arriving in the late 1890s, Samuel Q. O'Brien became Strathcona's leading lumber supplier, and by 1918 he joined the Strathcona gentry in building a home on Saskatchewan Drive. He chose a style that was then sweeping the western United States mass production home market, the California bungalow, with bellcast roof, wide veranda, stone

piers and an offset bay window.

Ritchie Mill
10170 Saskatchewan Dr.
Edmonton

The oldest surviving flour mill in Alberta is one of the few pre-1900 industrial buildings left. The Ritchie brothers, John and Robert, built it in 1892-93, and operated it as the Edmonton Milling Company, with easy access to the terminus of the Calgary and Edmonton Railway.

McKenzie/Galper Residence
8603 104 St.
Edmonton

John Walter's ferryman until 1891, blacksmith John James McKenzie later became a member of Strathcona's first school board, and was elected to council when Strathcona became a town in 1899. He was elected mayor in 1904 and built this house seven years later, just before the amalgamation of Strathcona with Edmonton at the height of the settlement boom.

Connaught Armories
10305 85 Ave.
Edmonton

Built in 1911 as the home of the 19th Alberta Dragoons, the Connaught Armories served one of the oldest militia groups in Alberta. Except for its recessed central bay and crenellated parapets, the brick bearing walls are more austere than the elaborate castle designs of other period armories.

Bard House
10544 84 Ave.
Edmonton

This fine Neo-Georgian private house was built in 1912 for Delmar Bard, a senior provincial government civil servant who experienced considerable success in real estate transactions. Its conservatory, carriage house and fine interior work support the assessment published in the Strathcona *Plaindealer* of June 7, 1912: "one of the best [homes] in the city."

Knox United Church
8403 104 St.
Edmonton

On the site of a Presbyterian mission begun with the assistance of Dr. D.G. McQueen about 1890, the new brick church designed by Magoon, Hopkins and James of Edmonton was dedicated in December, 1907. A good example of the Presbyterian use of Gothic Revival styles in that period, it was acquired by the Evangelical Free Church in 1972.

Strathcona Library
8331 104 St.
Edmonton

A Carnegie Foundation offer of $15,000 to establish this library was rejected so that Strathcona could demand a complete new south-south library as one of the conditions of amalgamation with Edmonton. Built in 1913 in an English Renaissance style created by Wilson and Herrald, it eventually cost Edmontonians $27,000.

Fire Hall Number Six
10322 83 Ave.
Edmonton

Built in 1909-10 for Strathcona's volunteer fire brigade, this is the oldest fire hall in Edmonton and one of the oldest in Alberta. After civic amalgamation in 1912, the brick building housed the Edmonton Fire Department until 1954. The asymmetrical tower contains Strathcona's original town bell.

Douglas Block
10442 82 Ave.
Edmonton

James and Robert Douglas established Douglas Brothers Department Store in 1899, and in 1912 constructed this large brick building designed by Wilson and Herrald. Each of the structure's three stories had a distinct function: stores on the ground floor, offices on the second, and apartments on the third.

Richards Block
10422 82 Ave.
Edmonton

The Richards Block was built in 1910 for A.E. Richards and Co., general merchant. The second floor was a dance hall, and the third held lodge rooms for the Masonic Lodge and the Oddfellows. After former premier A.C. Rutherford acquired it in 1925, the upper floors were converted into apartments.

Dominion Hotel
10322 82 Ave.
Edmonton

The hotel was built in 1903 by Robert McKernan, an early Edmonton settler who farmed in the Strathcona area. The ground floor originally included a lobby, dining hall and beer parlor, but the hotel was closed after the onset of provincial prohibition in 1915. The upper floors became apartments and the main floor was occupied by Backus Feed Store, the first of several tenants.

Strathcona Hotel
10302 82 Ave.
Edmonton

In 1891, the Calgary and Edmonton Railway Company completed construction of the Strathcona Hotel, the oldest wood-frame commercial building and the first hotel in Strathcona. Apart from a short period as Westminster Ladies College (1918-19), it has always been a hotel.

Chapman Brothers
10423 82 Ave.
Edmonton

Originally owned by Robert Ritchie, this small frame harness shop first operated under the name of the Great West Saddlery Co. A.B. Chapman rented the property in 1912 and bought it six years later. A.B. Chapman and Co., specializing in harnesses and leather goods, has remained as a family enterprise since the originator's death in the flu epidemic of 1918.

Gainer Block
10341 82 Ave.
Edmonton

John Gainer arrived in Strathcona on the first train to make the trip north from Calgary, in 1891. With no previous training as a butcher, but with a keen eye for the need, he opened his shop just west of the CPR tracks. The Gainer Block, opened in 1902, reflects the prosperity the meat-packing enterprise enjoyed for many years.

Princess Theatre
10335 82 Ave.
Edmonton

Built by John W. McKernan in 1914 at a cost of $75,000, this movie, vaudeville and musical concert theatre has a façade of British Columbia marble and a cornice of copper. The interior, decorated with plaster figures and friezes, remains close to the original design by Wilson and Herrald even today.

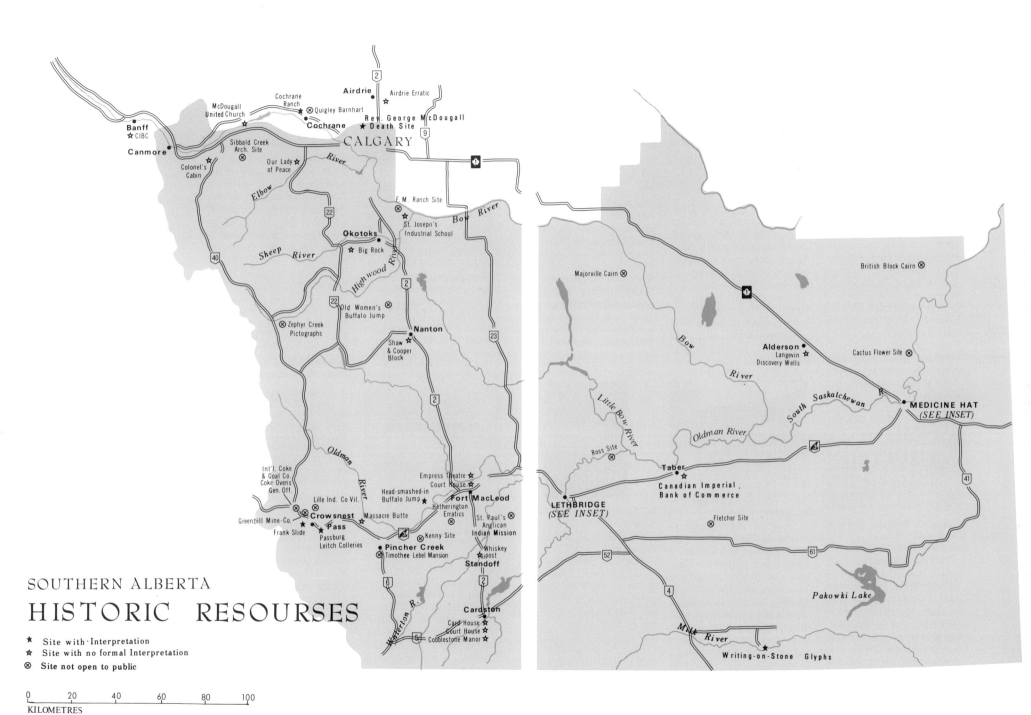

Airdrie ★ Airdrie Erratic

McDougall
United Church ☆
Cochrane
Ranch
☆ ⊗ Quigley Barnhart
Banff ● **Cochrane**
☆ CIBC
Rev. George McDougall
★ Death Site

Canmore ●
CALGARY
Sibbald Creek
Arch. Site
Colonel's ☆ ⊗
Cabin ☆ Our Lady
of Peace

F. M. Ranch Site
⊗

St. Josepn's
Industrial School
Okotoks ●
☆ Big Rock

Old Women's ⊗
Buffalo Jump
⊗ Zephyr Creek
Pictographs
Shaw ☆ **Nanton** ●
& Cooper
Block

Oldman
River
Int'l. Coke
& Coal Co.
Coke Ovens
Gen. Off.
⊗ Lille Ind. Co Vil.
⊗ Greenhill Mine Co. **Crowsnest** ⊗ Massacre Butte
Pass
Frank Slide ★
Passburg
Leitch Colleries
⊗ ● Kenny Site
⊗ Timothee Lebel Mansion
Pincher Creek ☆

Empress Theatre ☆
Court House ☆
Head-smashed-in
Buffalo Jump ★ **Fort MacLeod** ●
Hetherington
Erratics
St. Paul's ⊗
Anglican
Indian Mission
Whiskey
☆ post
Standoff ●

Cardston ●
Card House ⊗
Court House ☆
Cobblestone Manor ☆

Majorville Cairn ⊗

British Block Cairn ⊗

Alderson ●
Langevin
Discovery Wells

Cactus Flower Site ⊗

MEDICINE HAT ●
(SEE INSET)

Ross Site
⊗

Taber ●
☆
Canadian Imperial ,
Bank of Commerce

LETHBRIDGE
(SEE INSET)

Fletcher Site
⊗

Pakowki Lake

Writing-on-Stone Glyphs ★

SOUTHERN ALBERTA
HISTORIC RESOURSES

★ Site with·Interpretation
☆ Site with no formal Interpretation
⊗ Site not open to public

0   20   40   60   80   100
KILOMETRES

Ross Block
10313 82 Ave.
Edmonton

Built in 1894 by W.E. Ross, with an addition in 1903, this block was originally occupied by the Strathcona hardware business conducted by Ross and John Ferguson, and after 1897 by Ross alone. Its main floor has housed many enterprises over the years, including a restaurant and a flour mill. Upstairs, Ross Hall once flourished with art exhibitions, shows and touring performances.

Canadian Imperial Bank of Commerce
95 Banff Ave., Banff

This bank opened in Banff as the Canadian Imperial Bank in 1906. Most branch banks were built according to plans issued from head office, but this design, more resembling a log home than a commercial building, was considered more appropriate to the town's alpine setting.

Kananaskis Cabin/Colonel's Cabin
10 km southeast of Exshaw on Highway 40
0.5 km east of Barrier Lake

The Kananaskis Forest Experimental Station was built in 1936, as part of a relief work-camp for the unemployed. With the outbreak of war in 1939, it became first an internment camp for enemy aliens suspected of subversion and then in 1941 a German PoW camp. The camp commandant lived in this cabin.

Mine Manager's House
Canmore

In 1891 the American-based McNeill Bros. Coal Mines leased two Canadian mines, one of them in Canmore. W.F. McNeill came to this mine as mine manager in 1905. In 1907, he built his home, but the McNeill coal lease expired in 1912 and the manager moved away. Among the better-known occupants since then was Duncan McKinnon Crockford, the landscape artist.

Sibbald Creek Site
50 km west of Caglary, on Hwy. 968

At an early prehistoric campsite 10,000 years old, archaeological excavations have turned up fluted projectile points and other tools. The fluted point tradition is the earliest recognized in North America. The discoveries at Sibbald Creek suggest very early cultural connections between the peoples of the plains and mountain regions.

McDougall Memorial United Church
1.5 km East of Morley, off Hwy 1A

The first Methodist mission in southern Alberta was built in 1875-76. George, John and David McDougall all frequented or served here. The style is a vernacular "Carpenter's Gothic," with pointed windows and pinnacles. The tower is a later addition, marking the building's transition from a Methodist meeting house to a church.

Cochrane Ranche
1 km northwest of Cochrane, on Hwy 1A

Established in 1881, the Cochrane Ranche introduced large-scale ranching to Alberta, with cattle imported from Montana. Although two bitterly cold winters wiped out much of the livestock on the ranch's 100,000 acres, the Cochrane Ranche set the standard for similar successful enterprises at nearby locations.

Barnhart–Quigley House
204 Baird St.
Cochrane

James Quigley (1857-1930) was a Scottish-born miner who moved to Cochrane in 1883. In 1900, he opened Cochrane's first school. Within another decade, he owned and operated a brick factory and a sawmill. Quigley's home, built for him in 1889 by Charlie Pedeprat, is a rare eastern Canadian Gothic example. The original logs are still beneath the surface.

Our Lady of Peace Cairn
20 km west of Calgary, on the north bank of the Elbow River

The cairn erected by the Roman Catholic diocese of Calgary in 1939 commemorates the first permanent Roman Catholic mission to the Blackfoot. The square, rough log cabin was constructed in 1872 by Alexis Cardinal, and used by Father Leon Doucet and Father Constantine Scollen steadily until 1875, and less frequently until it was abandoned in 1882 in favour of other mission sites.

Zephyr Creek Pictographs
6 km southwest of Eden Valley, Highway 541

At the pictograph site, one of Alberta's largest, five panels display various prehistoric scenes, including the death of a bison hunter, other hunting scenes, religious themes and geometric designs, all painted on the rock in red pigment. The paintings show influences from the British Columbia plateau region and have proven an excellent source of information.

International Coal and Coke Co. General Office
0.5 km outside Coleman on Highway 3

The ornate detail of the International Coal and Coke Co.'s general office reflects the Company's prosperity and optimism in 1909, the year of its construction. The tall hip roof echoes the residential architecture typical of the area. The mine operated from 1903 to 1918, then again on a reduced basis from 1932 to 1952.

Greenhill Mine Complex
1 km north of Blairmore

West Canadian Collieries' development of the Greenhill Mine began in 1913 with the construction of a mine tipple. Along with the operations of the International Coal and Coke Co., Greenhill Mine established the Crowsnest Pass as a significant mining region of Canada, and encouraged the growth of several towns, including nearby Blairmore.

Frank Slide
Crowsnest Pass, between
Frank and Bellevue
One of the most catastrophic landslides to occur in Canada in historic times, the Frank Slide took 70 lives on the early morning of April 29, 1903. Above the mining town of Frank a huge limestone wedge slid from Turtle Mountain, crushing the local mine and the Canadian Pacific line through the Crowsnest Pass.

Leitch Collieries
4 km southeast of Bellevue
The businessmen who in 1907 opened the largest and most sophisticated Alberta coal mining and coking operation in the Crowsnest Pass were led by the Leitch family. Malcolm Leitch, company president, maintained crucial connections with the Canadian Pacific Railway market. Production peaked in 1913, but dwindling markets and capital forced closure in 1915.

Timothee Lebel Mansion
696 Kettle St., Pincher Creek
When Quebec-born Timothee Lebel moved into this mansion in 1909, he had spent 25 years in the merchandise business at Pincher Creek. The house, designed to combine French Canadian and New Orleans–style features, was donated to the Filles de Jesus in 1924 and became St. Vincent's Hospital.

Pump House Number Two
2140 9 Ave. SW
Calgary
Constructed in 1910, this was the second pump house in Calgary's waterworks system. Originally designed for manual operation, the pump house was eventually converted to an automatic boosting station. Service from this station was discontinued altogether in 1967, but after renovations, the building re-opened in 1974 as the Pump House Theatre.

Colonel James Walker House
Inglewood Bird Sanctuary
Calgary
Much of Calgary's early growth can be attributed to Colonel James Walker, the man who introduced both phone and mail services to the city, and whose sawmill supplied the lumber for many of the early frame buildings. The community of Inglewood is named after Walker's house, now run as a museum, in the midst of a bird sanctuary set up by the colonel's son.

Lacombe Home
146 Ave. and Macleod Tr.
Calgary
Built under the supervision of the pioneer missionary, Father Albert Lacombe in 1909, this was Alberta's first institution devoted to the care of the old and the orphaned. Father Lacombe lived here until his death in 1916, when the home passed to the ownership of the Sisters of Providence, who ran it for more than half a century.

Lille Industrial Complex
6 km north of Frank on
Highway 3
Lille was first prospected for coal in 1901. Two years later, J.J. Fluetot and C. Remy established West Canadian Collieries, with three mines close to Lille. During World War I the industry collapsed and today only the Bernard coking ovens remain from Lille's original 60 buildings.

Massacre Butte
3 km north of Cowley
Legend has it that a dozen men, women and children from Minnesota made their way between the Porcupine Hills and the Rockies as early as 1867. After they camped on a butte overlooking the Crowsnest River flats (a favoured Indian lookout), Blood Indian warriors led by Medicine Calf are said to have swept down on the intruders and wiped them out.

Kenney Site
Just south of Brocket on
Highway 3
This site represents the best campsite in southern Alberta for what is called Besant material. Besant projectile points date back to A.D. 100 to 800 and are heavy, often crudely worked, corner-notched points. Many stone and bone artifacts have been discovered here since excavation began in 1966.

William Nimmons House
1827 14 St. SW
Calgary
William Nimmons established himself as a rancher in the Calgary area about 1882. His varied business interests included a sandstone quarry, a commercial greenhouse, and real estate in what are now the Nob Hill and Bankview districts of the city. His Queen Anne-style home on the Bow River, with an encircling veranda and corner tower, reflects his prominence in early Calgary society.

Shaw Woollen Mill Site
Midnapore
Before leaving England in 1883, the Shaw family gathered together a complete line of woollen mill machinery. By 1890 they had opened the first woollen mill in Western Canada. Mrs. Shaw opened a store in Calgary specializing in men's suits made of cloth woven at the family mill. The mill burned to the ground in 1924.

St. Paul's Anglican Church
146 Ave. and Macleod Tr.
Calgary
An early settler, John Glenn, donated the land for this church, based on a smaller-scale version of the floor plan of the Anglican cathedral in Calgary. The church's first priest built his house halfway between these two parishes. In 1925, the church of St. Andrew the Apostle in the village of Thelveton in England donated an early 18th-century steeple bell to St. Paul's.

151

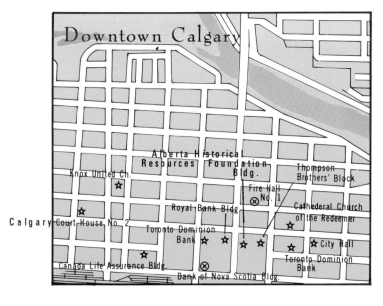

Downtown Calgary

Knox United Ch.

Alberta Historical Resources Foundation Bldg.

Thompson Brothers' Block

Fire Hall No. 1

Royal Bank Bldg.

Cathederal Church of the Redeemer

Calgary Court House No. 2

Toronto Dominion Bank

City Hall

Canada Life Assurance Bldg.

Toronto Dominion Bank

Bank of Nova Scotia Bldg.

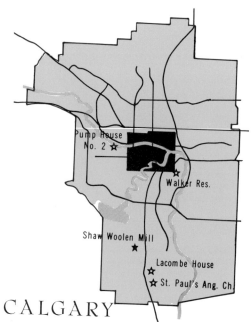

Pump House No. 2

Walker Res.

Shaw Woolen Mill

Lacombe House

St. Paul's Ang. Ch.

CALGARY

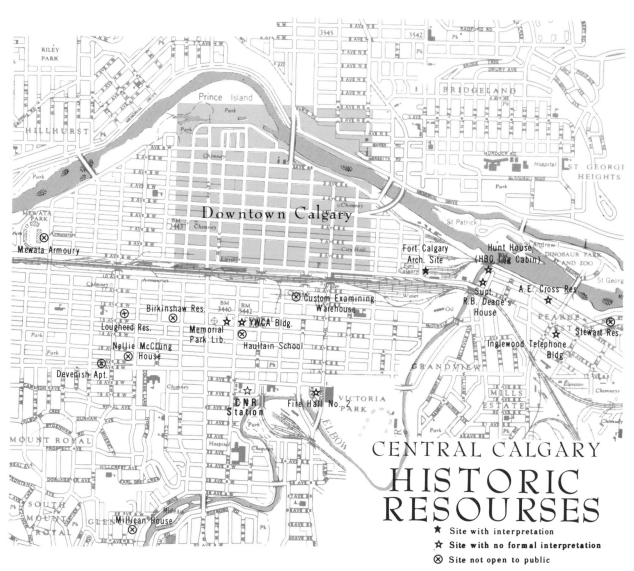

Downtown Calgary

Mewata Armoury

Fort Calgary Arch. Site

Hunt House (HBC Log Cabin)

A.E. Cross Res.

Custom Examining Warehouse

Supt. R.B. Deane's House

Birkinshaw Res.

Lougheed Res.

YWCA Bldg.

Memorial Park Lib.

Stewart Res.

Nellie McClung House

Haultain School

Inglewood Telephone Bldg.

Devenish Apt.

CNR Station

Fire Hall No. 2

Millican House

CENTRAL CALGARY

HISTORIC RESOURSES

★ Site with interpretation

☆ Site with no formal interpretation

⊗ Site not open to public

Knox United Church
506 4 St. SW
Calgary

The oldest church of Presbyterian origin in Calgary, Knox United was built from 1911 to 1913, incurring a debt that took the congregation more than 40 years to repay. Thirty-seven stained-glass windows commemorate members who died in World War I. The grand church's Casavant organ dates from 1913 and has more than 4,000 pipes.

Calgary Courthouse
530 7 Ave. SW
Calgary

Designed to replace an earlier courthouse, this two-storey structure built between 1912 and 1914 is part of Calgary's ''Sandstone City'' legacy. It served as the city's courthouse for 48 years, and afterwards housed the Glenbow Museum until 1976.

Canada Life Assurance Building
301 8 Ave. SW
Calgary

A product of Calgary's 1912 boom, this building was one of the most substantial in the downtown core in its day. The only Alberta example of design by the Montreal firm of Brown and Vallance, the building's form owes much to the influence of the U.S. architect Louis Henry Sullivan. The familiar Canada Life terra cotta facade is retained on the new structure behind.

Bank of Nova Scotia Building
125 8 Ave. SW
Calgary

Constructed in 1930, this is Alberta's only example of the work of John M. Lyle, for many years the chief architect with the Bank of Nova Scotia. Lyle is best remembered for his blending of classical style with Canadian themes, seen here in low-relief carved panels depicting agriculture and ranching, many of them ac-

tually carved by Lyle himself.

Molson's/Toronto Dominion Bank
114 8 Ave. SW
Calgary

Built for Molson's Bank in 1912, this building was purchased by the Bank of Montreal in the 1930s, then acquired by the Toronto Dominion in 1950 and renovated in 1980. In contrast to the flat, more restrained classical architecture of the city's sandstone buildings, the Eighth Avenue Toronto Dominion has high relief surfaces and borrows baroque elements for its detailing.

Royal Bank Building
102 8 Ave. SW
Calgary

Here stood the first Hudson's Bay Company store, torn down in 1889 to make way for a larger structure. After expansion in 1895 and 1905, the building was acquired by the Royal Bank. Rare features amidst the

more typical rough sandstone construction of early Calgary are this building's dressed sandstone columns and cornices.

Alberta Historical Resources Foundation Building
102 8 Ave. SE
Calgary

I.G. Baker and Co., the fur-trading organization, started business on this location in the late 1880s, later to be bought out by the Hudson's Bay Company. In 1910 the Imperial Bank of Canada established its branch and maintained it here until 1972.

Fire Hall Number One
6 Ave. and 1 St. SE
Calgary

Constructed in 1911 as the headquarters of the Calgary Fire Department, this brick and sandstone building replaced earlier headquarters dating from 1887. The fire hall was built to face

onto the street at an angle, allowing fire trucks to make quick exits in all directions.

Thomson Brothers Block
112 8 Ave. SW, Calgary

Thomson Brothers conducted a stationery business when this building opened in 1893. After 1900 the building was occupied by a succession of other retailers. The designer's complete disregard of accepted architechtural conventions (for example, variations in sandstone textures, stone height and window shapes) demonstrated the decorative extremes to which vernacular architecture could go during the earliest stages of western urban development.

Cathedral Church of the Redeemer
210 7 Ave. SE
Calgary

The Cathedral Church of the Redeemer has been the centre of Calgary's Anglican diocese since 1889. This particular church replaced the original in 1905. Its Gothic Revival design leans heavily on German medieval

models, and was one of the first in Calgary to incorporate buttresses as part of its support system.

Dominion Bank Building
200 8 Ave. SE
Calgary

This was the head office of the Dominion Bank in Calgary, before its merger with the Bank of Toronto. The building, from the period of the great bank expansion before World War I, displays the elaborate Beaux-Arts design planned by G.W. Northwood, with its facade of terra cotta, sandstone and marble, the heavy use of molding, and elaborate soffit decoration

Calgary City Hall
716 Macleod Tr. SE
Calgary

The site of this building, constructed between 1907 and 1911, has been the seat of Calgary's civic administration since 1885. Once described as the most modern city hall west of Toronto, the design won a prize for its architect,

William Dodd, of Dodd and Hopkins, though it cost more than twice its originally estimated price.

Mewata Armory
801 11 St. SW
Calgary

Well before World War I, the Dominion government launched plans for military training establishments. During the war, Calgary donated Mewata Park as a site for its armory. The vast open space in the main hall has since its 1917 construction accommodated track meets and charity bazaars as well as the training of soldiers and cadets.

Sir James Lougheed's Residence
707 13 Ave. SW
Calgary

Sir James Lougheed (1854-1925) practised law in Toronto and Calgary, where he was legal counsel for the Canadian Pacific Railway. Conservative leader in the Senate from 1906 to 1921, he also held several Cabinet

posts, and was knighted in 1917 by King George V. "Beaulieu" was built in 1891 to a design that borrows from Victorian, French chateau and eclectic Greek styles.

Devenish Apartments
904 17 Ave. SW
Calgary

Oscar G. Devenish built these apartments in 1911 from a design by Calgary architect Alexander Pirie at a cost of $200,000, a vast sum in those days. The overriding theme was elegance, and to lure potential tenants the Devenish offered built-in furniture, telephones and beautiful bay windows.

Nellie McClung House
803 15 Ave. SW
Calgary

Nellie McClung, author, lecturer, prohibitionist and feminist, lived in this expansive, half-timbered home from 1923-1935, before her retirement to Victoria, B.C. The house, described in her autobiography *The Stream*

Runs Fast, was her home during her participation in the celebrated "Person's Case" in which she and four other women successfully pressed for recognition of women as "persons" eligible for Senate appointment.

Millican House
3015 Glencoe Rd. SW
Calgary

William J. Millican built this home in 1914 and the Nickle family, well known for oil industry enterprise, acquired it in 1930. It was known as "Olga House" after Sam Nickle's wife, who loved to entertain here. In this combination of Edwardian and Queen Anne styling, each floor has a different window style: Palladian on the ground floor, square-headed and round-headed on first and second stories.

Birkinshaw Residence
621 13 Ave. SW
Calgary

This handsome brick home with sandstone trim and diamond-pane leaded glass dates to Calgary's

major growth period before World War I. Among its locally prominent owners before the war was Oris S. Chapin, whose company dealt in farm equipment and repaired some of Calgary's earliest Ford automobiles.

Memorial Park Library
1221 2 St. SW
Calgary

Completed in 1912 from plans prepared by Boston architects, Memorial Park Library was only the second library built between Winnipeg and the Rockies. Like others in Western Canada, its funding came in part from the Carnegie Foundation. Between 1963 and 1977, the building housed the Glenbow-Alberta Institute's library and archives.

Old YWCA Building
223 12 Ave. SW
Calgary

Alberta's first YWCA was built in Calgary in 1910-11. It played a prominent role in providing housing, educational activities and social and cultural pursuits for

women newly arrived to the city. In 1912 the YWCA opened an employment bureau, in recognition of the increasing importance of women in the Canadian workforce.

Haultain School
225 13 Ave. SW
Calgary

Built around 1892, this is the oldest standing school in Calgary and the first of a trend to build all city schools of local sandstone. The building is named after Frederick W.G. Haultain (1857-1942), member for Fort Macleod in the Territorial Legislature (1887-1905), and Premier of the N.W.T. from 1897 to 1905.

Customs Examining Warehouse
134 11 Ave. SE
Calgary

In the service of the federal government since 1915, this brick and sandstone four-storey structure demonstrates the talents of federal architect David

Ewart. His design imposed traditional Renaissance Revival segmented arches with keystones, modified doric columns, resticated sandstone base and iron cornice on a modern Chicago School structural grid steel frame.

CNR Station
18 Ave. and 1 St. SW
Calgary

Calgary's CNR station began life as St. Mary's Parish Hall, built for the Oblate order in 1905 by architect James O'Hara. In 1911 the Canadian Northern Railway (later absorbed by the Canadian National Railway) bought the hall and converted it into a station.

Fire Hall Number Two/Police Station
1807 Macleod Tr. SE
Calgary

Fire Hall Number Two replaced a smaller frame structure during Calgary's building boom in 1912. Until the end of World War I it accommodated both fire hall and police station, then con-

154

tinued as a fire hall until 1976.

Fort Calgary
700 Block on 9 Ave. SE
Calgary

In 1875 Inspector E.A. Brisebois and his detachment of North West Mounted Police arrived at the junction of the Bow and Elbow rivers and supervised the construction of a fort, including two large barracks, quartermaster's store, stables and a palisade outer wall for protection. There the divisional headquarters of the Mounted Police remained until 1914.

Hunt House
890 9 Ave. S.E.
Calgary

The oldest structure in Calgary still on its original site, "Hunt House" was built on the east side of the Elbow River between 1876 and 1881. The one-room cabin's location, across from the site of the N.W.M.P. Fort Calgary, leaves open the possibility that the Hudson's Bay Company's interpreter occupied the house.

Superintendent R.B. Deane House
806 9 Ave. SE
Calgary

The only building left from the North West Mounted Police occupation of Fort Calgary, it was described in 1906 by Superintendent R. Burton Deane as "the best house in Mounted Police occupancy." In 1914 the Grand Trunk Pacific Railway bought the property and moved the house for use by the station agent. In 1929 it was floated across the Elbow River for apartment accommodation.

A.E. Cross House
1240 8 Ave. SE
Calgary

Alfred Ernest Cross (1861-1932) was born in Montreal and moved west in his early twenties to take up the life of a rancher. His Calgary house was built in 1891, just before he founded the Calgary Brewing and Malting Company in 1892. An early investor in the Turner Valley oil and natural gas fields, Cross served in

the Northwest Territories government, and was one of the "Big Four" who launched the Calgary Stampede.

Stewart House
26 New St. SE
Calgary

Major John Stewart (1854-93) built his home at the original Calgary townsite in 1884-85, just before the former military officer organized the Rocky Mountain Rangers for the protection of southern Alberta settlers against the threat of the Northwest Rebellion. Stewart's business interests ranged from coal mines to stagecoaches.

Inglewood Telephone Building
1311 9 Ave. SE
Calgary

Colonel James Walker brought the telephone to Calgary in 1887. While initially slow to catch on, demand for phone service had become so great by 1909 that the main switchboard was replaced by the city's first automatic exchange system. By 1910, all 300 lines into the

Inglewood Telephone Building were in use, and its capacity was expanded and fitted into the Calgary telephone system until 1957.

Airdrie Erratic
3 km east of Airdrie

Part of the Foothills Erratics Train is located on a farm north of Sharp Hill. Where glaciers from the Rockies near Jasper were deflected southward by the massive Laurentide ice sheet 50,000 years ago, an "erratic train" of rocks was deposited. The Airdrie Erratic is bedded quartzite with Indian pictographs on its surface.

Rev. George McDougall Death Site
In North Calgary, 6 km west of Beddington

Methodist missionary George McDougall spent the last 16 years of his life spreading the Christian gospel in Canada's west. After building the first Methodist church in Edmonton in 1873, he moved south to Morley to build another. On a bitterly cold January

night in 1876, he failed to return from a buffalo hunt, and his body was found here.

F.M. Ranch Site
19 km southeast of Calgary, 13 km east of Highway 2 on Highway 522

One of many prehistoric campsites in Alberta, the F.M. Ranch Site is unusual for its close proximity to a buffalo jump. Excavation in 1974 revealed a number of occupation horizons dating to around A.D. 1000, each with well-defined quantities of butchered bone, stone implements and rock that had been broken by the heat of a domestic fire.

St. Joseph's Industrial School
15 km northeast of Okotoks, on Highway 2

Father Albert Lacombe built this school in 1884 to give local Blackfoot and Cree boys occupational education with a firm basis in agriculture. After a slow initial response, enrollment eventually reached around 150, and the school won prizes

for its pedigree livestock and produce before it closed in 1919. No buildings remain and the school site is marked with a commemorative cairn.

Big Rock
10 km west of Okotoks, on Highway 7

The nearby town of Okotoks derives its name from the Blackfoot word *Okatok*, for "the rock." This huge glacial erratic, weighing some 16,000 tonnes, is the largest in the Foothills Erratics Train stretching from Jasper to Montana. The erratics were probably deposited by a glacier advancing eastward and southward from a rock slide in the Rocky Mountains perhaps 50,000 years ago.

Old Women's Buffalo Jump
3.5 km northwest of Cayley on Highway 540

Of the two Blackfoot buffalo jumps bearing this name, this one is believed to be the oldest of all the Blackfoot jumps and an archaeological treasure. According to legend, it got its name when Napi (creator of the world's wonders) suggested to men that they get together and live with women in one camp.

Shaw and Cooper Block
Nanton

When the Calgary and Edmonton Railway Company founded the town of Nanton at a place previously called Mosquito Creek, H.M. Shaw left his ranching experience to open the community's first store. J.T. Cooper was Nanton's first mayor. The names of these two early business pioneers are remembered in the block that they had built for them in 1909, and which survived as an integral part of downtown Nanton.

Majorville Cairn
38 km west of Brooks south of Highway 1

At this site on the banks of the Bow River, a large cairn made of fieldstones rests in the centre of a medicine wheel. Building the cairn began some time around

3200 B.C. and continued until the arrival of Euro-Canadians. The site was a ceremonial place perhaps associated with the hunting of the plains bison, but little more than that is known.

British Block Cairn
Suffield Military Reserve, 60 km north of Medicine Hat, 35 km west of Highway 41

As tall as a person and 10 m across, this cairn on a hill above the shortgrass plains was made up of tonnes of rock ranging in size from pebbles to boulders weighing 200 kg and more. A large medicine wheel encircles the cairn, which is believed to date back to 3,000 BC.

Cactus Flower Site
Southeast corner of Suffield Military Reserve, 20 km north of Medicine Hat

The major example of a "McKean phase" campsite in Alberta, the Cactus Flower Site is from the Middle prehistoric period 6500 BC to AD 200-700). It is a large site, by Canadian plains standards, and has provided a host of finds—in-

cluding ash-filled, basin-shaped hearths and projectile points — since excavations began in 1971.

Langevin Gas Wells
15 km northwest of Suffield on Highway 1

In 1883, at what was then known as Langevin (now Alderson), a drilling crew working under contract to the C.P.R. struck natural gas instead of the water they sought. When Langevin Number One caught fire the following year, another well was drilled and it began a production which lasted until the mid-1930s.

Canadian Imperial Bank of Commerce
5227 48 Ave., Taber

This Bank of Commerce built in 1912 typifies the two-storey brick and stone structures built in smaller centres during the great expansion era of 1900 to 1914, with neoclassical details like the four partial columns on the front facade and carved stone window and door surrounds.

Fletcher Site
25 km southwest of Grassy Lake, 8 km north of Highway 61

Alberta's first-discovered Early Man site was excavated in 1963. The site contains some of the oldest cultural components yet discovered in the Alberta plains. These date back more than 7,000 years. The bones of extinct buffalo, as well as stone and bone tools, have been recovered at the Fletcher Site.

Ross Site
East of Lethbridge, south of the Little Bow River

Excavated in 1957, the Ross Site is a prehistoric campsite believed to date back to A.D. 1,000. Archaeologists found a wide range of artifacts: pottery in several different styles, bone tools and some artifacts made of stone. A supply of wood loaded nearby indicates repeated use for winter camping.

Empress Theatre
235 24 St., Fort Macleod

The Empress Theatre was built as a vaudeville theatre in 1912. As signatures on the dressing room walls attest, the Empress drew acts from as far away as California, New York, and Australia. Its many remaining original features include the decorative stucco panels, a pressed tin ceiling and a roll-down mountain scenery backdrop.

Fort Macleod Courthouse
234 23 St., Fort Macleod

Built between 1902 and 1904, this is the only remaining western Canadian example of the Dominion government's standard court design, and the last surviving building that served both the territorial and the Alberta governments. In 1910, a large assembly of Blood Indians gathered on the courthouse grounds to greet Sir Wilfrid Laurier.

Head-Smashed-In Buffalo Jump
15 km west of Fort Macleod, on Highway 785

In 1981 UNESCO placed Head-Smashed-In Buffalo Jump on its World Heritage List in recognition of 5,500 years of communal bison hunting at this complex site. It has three distinct parts: the basin, where the animals gathered to graze; the kill site or jump, to which the hunters herded the bison between lines of stone cairns; and finally the campsite below, where the butchering was done.

Hetherington Erratics Fields
21 km southeast of Fort Macleod

Fifty thousand years ago advancing glacial ice left behind rocks moved from their original place, called "erratics." The Hetherington Erratics Field contains 12 major erratics and several smaller ones, a high concentration explained by the steep hill to the west which restricted the movement of the glacier.

St. Paul's Anglican Indian Mission
19 km southeast of Fort Macleod

The pioneer Anglican missionary, the Rev. Samuel Trivett, began his mission to the Blood Indians in 1880 on behalf of the Missionary Society of the Church of England in Canada. The first boarders at the school built in 1882 were in residence in 1889. Of the dozen buildings which once included a church complete with bell tower, only the girls' school, completed in 1891, still stands.

Cardston Courthouse
89-3 Ave. SW, Cardston

Under the suggestion of Alberta Public Works provincial architect A.M. Jeffers, Cardston contractor Samuel S. Newton built and may have collaborated in designing Alberta's first provincial courthouse between 1906 and 1909. The heavily massed building is the oldest in Alberta to see continuous use as a courthouse.

Card Home
337 Main St., Cardston

Charles Ora Card was a Mormon founder and first mayor of the town of Cardston. He oversaw development of the extensive local irrigation system, corn mill, sawmill, cheese factory and the Cardston Mercantile Company that laid the commercial and agricultural basis of the town. Card's 1883 log home was dismantled, cleaned and reassembled in 1937.

Fort Stand Off
1 km west of Stand Off, on Highway 810

In 1871, illegal whiskey traders faced a U.S. Marshall, who had caught up with them at the Milk River and ordered them to return to face justice in the United States. Because the smugglers claimed immunity in Canada, the result was a "stand off." The whiskey trading "fort" was abandoned with the arrival of the North West Mounted Police in 1874.

Cobblestone Manor
173 7 Ave. W, Cardston

Joseph Young, sent to Cardston in 1893 by the Church of Jesus Christ of Latter-Day Saints, built a two-storey log house and sold it to Henry Hoet, a carpenter working on the Mormon temple in Cardston. Hoet applied cobblestone to the facade and used exotic imported woods left over from the temple's construction, skilfully carved, for furniture production and interior finishing work.

Writing-On-Stone Glyphs
40 km east of Milk River

In and outside of Writing-On-Stone Provincial Park, petroglyphs (carved designs) and pictographs (painted designs) as old as 3,000 years abound in thousands of panels, each containing designs of deep religious significance for native peoples. Small prehistoric camp workshops, tipi rings, a burial site and a North West Mounted Police post are nearby.

Blackfoot–Cree Indian Battle
1 km west of Lethbridge, on Highway 25

In the fall of 1870, some 800 Cree and Assiniboine warriors crossed the Oldman River and launched an attack on their Blood and Blackfoot enemies. As they were driven back into the river, between 200 and 300 warriors perished in the last major intertribal battle in what is now Alberta. Stone cairns commemorate the dead.

Sir Alexander Galt Museum
5 Ave. S, Lethbridge

Sir Alexander Galt, one of the founding fathers of Confederation and Canada's first finance minister, is associated with development of the western coal industry, irrigation and railroad work. The museum was originally a hospital Galt established in 1910 for the miners who had worked for his Alberta Railway and Coal Co.

Fire Hall Number One
402 2 Ave. S, Lethbridge

One of the oldest brick fire halls still standing in Alberta, this 1908-09 model also housed civic administration offices and a police station. The fire hall closed in 1974, but its Classic Revival architecture and prominent dome make it a well-known Lethbridge landmark.

C.A. Magrath Residence
109 7th Ave. S, Lethbridge

In 1885, C.A. Magrath moved to Lethbridge as a surveyor and land agent. A man of considerable influence, he later became first president of the Lethbridge Board of Trade, Lethbridge's first mayor and a member of the prestigious Royal Society of Canada. Magrath built "Valleyview" in 1892. The original design and facade have remained prominent through later renovations.

Bowman Arts Centre
811 5 Ave. S, Lethbridge

Built in 1912 as the Lethbridge Manual Training Centre, this was Alberta's first technical school, and then a high school (1915 to 1963). It later became a community arts centre, named after Charles B. Bowman, one-time director of the Lethbridge Board of Trade and a local alderman.

Hardie Residence
1242 5 Ave. S, Lethbridge

W.D.L. Hardie was colliery superintendent for Sir Alexander Galt's Alberta Railway and Coal Co. and went on to become mayor of Lethbridge from 1913 to 1928. Hardie's prominent Georgian home with its classically inspired details reflects his status in the community and the traditional pre-World War I practice of mixing historical architectural styles.

157

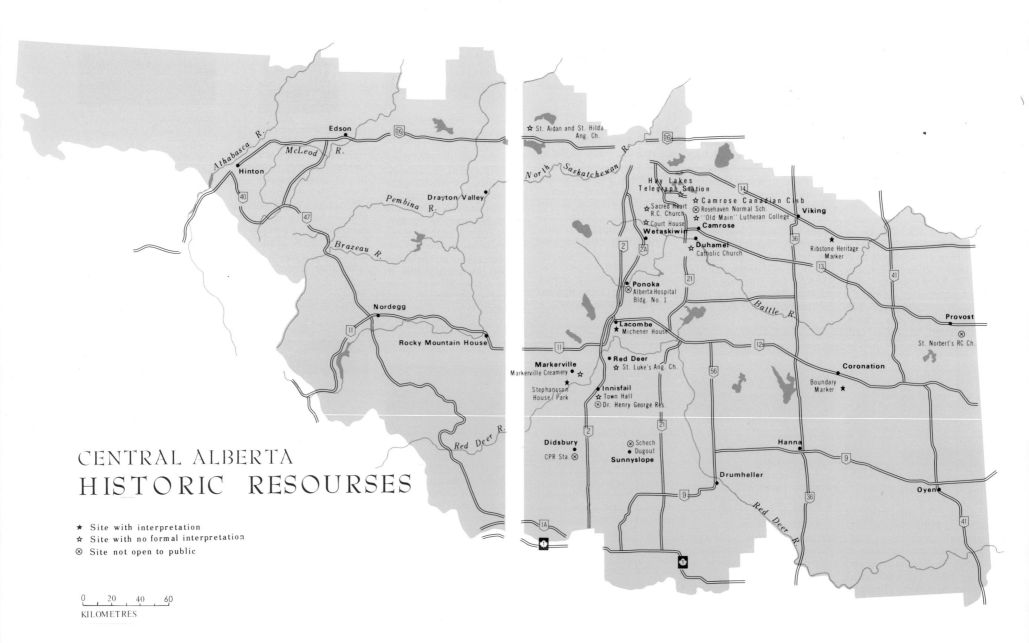

CENTRAL ALBERTA
HISTORIC RESOURSES

★ Site with interpretation
☆ Site with no formal interpretation
⊗ Site not open to public

0   20   40   60
KILOMETRES

Edson

Athabasca R.

McLeod R.

Hinton

Pembina R.

Drayton Valley

Brazeau R.

Nordegg

Rocky Mountain House

Red Deer R.

☆ St. Aidan and St. Hilda Ang. Ch.

North Saskatchewan R.

Hay Lakes Telegraph Station

☆ Camrose Canadian Club

☆ Sacred Heart R.C. Church
⊗ Rosehaven Normal Sch.
☆ "Old Main" Lutheran College

Viking

☆ Court House
Wetaskiwin

Camrose

☆ Duhamel Catholic Church

Ribstone Heritage Marker ★

Ponoka
⊗ Alberta Hospital Bldg. No. 1

Battle R.

Provost

Lacombe
★ Michener House

⊗ St. Norbert's RC Ch.

Red Deer
☆ St. Luke's Ang. Ch.

Coronation

Markerville
Markerville Creamery ● ☆

Stephansson House Park ★

● **Innisfail**
☆ Town Hall
⊗ Dr. Henry George Res.

Boundary Marker ★

Didsbury

CPR Sta. ⊗

⊗ Schech Dugout

Hanna

Sunnyslope

Drumheller

Red Deer R.

Oyen

Medicine Hat Courthouse
460 1 St. SE, Medicine Hat

Built in 1919-1920, this courthouse proved influential in the design of two others in Red Deer and Vegreville. The Beaux-Arts Classical style, with its L-shaped floor plan and Spanish roof, had been popular in the United States, but is rarer in western Canada. The roof originally bore Spanish tiles.

Canadian Imperial Bank of Commerce
577 2 Ave. SE, Medicine Hat

Medicine Hat went through a building boom after 1900, with the discovery of natural gas and coal deposits in the area, and the influx of agricultural settlers. In 1907, the Canadian Bank of Commerce replaced an older, wood-frame bank with this, the city's first permanent bank building.

Medalta Potteries
Industrial Ave. - Medalta Ave. Medicine Hat

One of the oldest surviving potteries in Canada, Medalta was the first western Canadian firm to ship manufactured goods east of the Lakehead. After 1921, Medalta cornered the Canadian stoneware market and by the 1940s handled all the important contracts, including those with C.P.R. and C.N.R. The plant closed in the late 1960s.

St. Aidan and Hilda Anglican Church
At Rexboro, 56 km west of Edmonton, near Whitewood Lake

Associated with the pre-World War I settlement of Alberta, St. Aidan and Hilda Church was consecrated in 1911. Built of tamarack logs, on land donated by homesteader Harry Smith, it was to serve as a religious and community focus for the district's English settlers. The church's bell came from England and was placed in the belfry in 1917.

Hay Lakes Telegraph Station
2 km east of Hay Lakes townsite

Until 1879 the telegraph lines ended at this telegraph station, rather than at Edmonton. James McKernan and his brother Robert operated it. The first message was transmitted on November 20, 1877, from Major Jarvis of the North-West Mounted Police at Fort Saskatchewan to Battleford.

Sacred Heart Church
1 km west of Wetaskiwin

The pioneer missionaries, fathers Lacombe and Leduc, both celebrated mass in this church, built in 1894. It served in succession as church, priest's residence, schoolroom for the town's first Roman Catholic school, and even a Lutheran congregation's church until 1966. The church was the moved to the Sacred Heart Cemetery.

Wetaskiwin Courthouse
4705 50 Ave., Wetaskiwin

The town of Wetaskiwin is the centre of Alberta's central judicial district. In 1907, as part of the judicial organization in the new province, a handsome sandstone and brick courthouse was erected with classical Greek features like the portico to emphasize permanence and importance. The two field cannons were captured from the Germans in World War I.

Camrose Canadian Club
4859 50 St., Camrose

Originally built in 1908 as the home of the Camrose Canadian Club, an independent organization of local businessmen, it had a reading room and a billiards room for members. Sold in 1918, the building has had many occupants in such roles as courthouse, Treasury Branch and public library. Its form recalls the optimism and interest of the city's founders.

Rosehaven (Camrose Normal School)
4612 53 St., Camrose

Built in 1915 as a normal school, or teachers' college, this structure is one of the province's rare examples of the "Collegiate Gothic" style of re-creating the appearance of an "old" place of learning. The building was used as a basic training centre during World War II, and was later converted to a mental-health centre for the elderly called "Rosenhaven."

"Old Main," Camrose Lutheran College
4901 46 Ave., Camrose

The first building at Camrose Lutheran College, "Old Main" was designed by its first principal, J.P. Tandberg, and built in 1912. The college has always been closely associated with Norwegian settlers of the area. Chester Ronning, later to serve as Canadian ambassador to China (1942-49), was a student here, then returned as the college's principal.

St. Thomas Duhamel Church
13 km southwest of Camrose, on Highway 21

St. Thomas is typical of the mission-church "Carpenter Gothic" architectural design in the west. It was built in 1893, of post-and-sill construction, chinked with moss. In 1915, a steeple and sacristy were built, the log church was re-sided, and the church's bell was donated by Archbishop Joseph-Thomas Duhamel.

Ribstone Heritage Monument
27 km east of Viking

Ribstones are large boulders (usually glacial in origin) whose surfaces the native people have chipped to form designs, frequently of the ribs and backbones of animals. The stones are believed to be connected with worship centres that date back long before the arrival of white settlers, possibly in ceremonies enacted to ensure successful bison hunts.

Alberta Hospital Building Number One
2 km south of Ponoka on Highway 2A

The first building in Alberta specifically designed for the treatment of mental illness opened in 1911. Its layout was modelled after an acute care hospital in Utica, New York. Later additions to the hospital included cottages, craft workshops and halfway houses.

St. Norbert's Roman Catholic Church
3.5 km east of Provost

St. Norbert's was built between 1922 and 1926, on the site of a 1908 predecessor, to serve the district's large German-Canadian population. Its German Baroque dome attests to its cultural origin. The spire, almost 60 m high, was later used as a landmark by military pilot trainees.

Stephansson House
30 km west of Red Deer, near Markerville on Highway 54

Born in Iceland in 1853, farmer-poet Stephan G. Stephansson came to western Canada (via North Dakota) in 1889. His home was built in stages, finally completed in 1907. Invited back to his homeland in 1917, he was hailed as Iceland's greatest poet since the 13th century. Most of his poetry was written in this country farmhouse.

Markerville Creamery
Markerville

In 1899 the Canadian government bought out two ailing cheese factories west of the Red Deer River and encouraged 36 local Icelandic farmers to found the Tindastoll Butter and Cheese Manufacturing Association. Around the successful creamery grew the village of Markerville, as butter production almost quadrupled between 1900 and 1923. The creamery closed in 1969.

Dr. Henry George's Home
5711 51 Ave., Innisfail

Innisfail's first doctor, Dr. Henry George had his home built in 1893. His passion for natural history was revealed in his collection of everything from stuffed birds to Indian artifacts. Dr. George was vitally interested in heritage preservation, and was president of the Alberta Natural History Society several times between 1905 and 1913.

Schech Dugout
25 km west of Three Hills

Erich C. Steendahl took up this homestead in 1902 but left in 1903. While he may have built the dugout, it seems more likely that George Schech, a stonemason who came to the homestead from Wisconsin in 1904, built in the stone steps, mortared walls and domed roof. He lived in this earth-sheltered home for some time.

Roland Michener Home
5036 51 St., Lacombe

Built in 1894 as the parsonage of the Lacombe Methodist Church, the fame of this turn-of-the-century home arises from its connection with one of Canada's Governors-General. It was here that Roland Michener was born, before launching a career as Rhodes scholar, Oxford graduate, lawyer, politician, and ultimately Governor-General of Canada (1963-73).

St. Luke's Anglican Church
4929 44 St., Red Deer

The Edmonton architectural firm of W.S. Edmiston and H.D. Johnson joined the Rev. Joshua Hinchcliffe—an outstanding clergyman who gave up a promising career as a architect in England to come to Canada as an Anglican priest—in designing this Gothic Revival Church made of local sandstone. The cornerstone was laid in September, 1899; construction took eight years.

Stephansson Park
Markerville

In 1953, the centenary of poet Stephan G. Stephansson's birth, the federal government's Historic Sites and Monuments Board erected a cairn on ground adjacent to Markerville's community park. The park itself, including the provincial historic site, is where Icelandic Day celebrations are held on the Saturday closest to June 17 each year.

Innisfail Town Hall
5004 50 St., Innisfail

This town hall began as a branch of the Union Bank of Canada. Built in 1914, its heavily-detailed style is typical of bank design of the period, which was aimed at creating the illusion of stability and permanence. The Union Bank merged with the Royal Bank in 1925.

Didsbury CPR Station
Opposite the Didsbury grain elevators on Highway 582

Alberta's only remaining railway station with a mansard roof was built in 1902. Like most small-town railway stations, it fulfilled several functions: not only was it a depot and travellers' shelter, but it had telegraph facilities. A freight shed was later added to the rear of the building.

Coronation Boundary Marker
12 km south of Coronation

In 1882, the Canadian government divided part of the huge Northwest Territories into provisional districts with defined boundaries. Three of those districts met here, south of Coronation: Alberta to the west, Saskatchewan to the northeast, and Assiniboia to the southeast. A provincial cairn marks the intersection point.